FLIGHT AND RETURN:

A MEMOIR OF WORLD WAR II

ALSO BY MAXIMILIAN LERNER

Fiction

The Expendable Spy
The Improbable Spy

FLIGHT AND RETURN:
A MEMOIR OF WORLD WAR II

MAXIMILIAN LERNER

Lerner

"The only thing necessary for the triumph of evil is for good men to do nothing."

— Edmund Burke

DEDICATION

First and foremost to Lenore who has made the second half of my life a constant joy.

Then to all of my children and all of my grandchildren with a special warning to the latter: You are accustomed to hearing fanciful tales of pirates, knights, cowboys and Indians from your grandpa, this book, alas, contains only the truth as well as I can recall it.

And to the Jewish People, stubborn in their desire to live the way they want to live. Surviving the Roman Empire, the Byzantine Empire, the crusaders, the Inquisition, the Cossacks, the most brutal and destructive efforts by that civilized nation Germany that reduced their numbers by a third, and that seductive and constant threat – assimilation. And they returned to their ancient land after 2000 years of exile and created a home.

I am proud to be a member of this people.

CONTENTS

PROLOGUE

The MP brought in the next prisoner.

This was the first time that I dealt with a high-ranking member of the SS. The prisoner stood slumped over with a hangdog look, while I inspected him leisurely. He wore the standard SS uniform, with the death's head insignia, and his rank was indicated by the pips on his collar. It seemed as if his tunic was too big for him, or had he shrunk because he was at the other end of the interrogation table?

He had no hat, and the collar buttons were open. His boots were unpolished. He was far from the dapper and elegant SS officers who used to lord it over the general population.

An intense feeling of hatred rose within me. This was the man, or someone like him, who was responsible for untold crimes against humanity, and in particular against me. And now, he was in my power. I felt like jumping up and smashing his face in.

Instead, I said with all the calm I could muster: "Sit down, Sturmbannfuehrer (Major). Tell me all about yourself."

CHAPTER 1

WARNING:

These first two chapters deal with my ancestry and my family. Those of you, dear Readers, who are only interested in my memoirs of World War II, may wish to begin with Chapter Three.

***

At the Holocaust Museum in Washington, D.C. there is a bridge, reminiscent of the bridge that connected the two parts of the Warsaw Ghetto. Engraved on the glass walls of the bridge are the names of the many communities in Europe that housed vibrant, Jewish lives and that are no more.

Among those names are listed three of particular significance to our family- Halicz, Rozniatov and Stanislawow.

My father was born in Halicz, my mother in Rozniatow, and Stanislawow was the county seat where, for all I know, they met.

My father, Isak Lerner, was born on November 23, 1889. His father, my grandfather, had the honored name of Moshe – Moses. I never met him. He died before I was born. I was told that he was born in 1870 in Stzeliska and that he was an innkeeper. I carry his name.

His wife, my grandmother, was born Regina Auster. She was born in 1874 in Galukier. I never met her either. She was sickly and never travelled to Vienna, Austria, where we lived, nor did we ever go to visit her, although my father visited her frequently on his numerous business trips. I remember that she died while my father was traveling. Usually, when my father returned from a business trip, my sister and I would run to meet him at the front door. In this case, my mother told us to wait so that she could meet him alone to give him the news.

I do not know exactly when this occurred. I assume that I was no more than seven or eight years old.

My mother, Bertha Lerner, nee Deutscher, was born in Rozniatov on May 20, 1890. Her father, my grandfather, was Uri (Ire) Zweifler – I do not know his birthdate or his place of origin. He died in Vienna on August 24, 1937 of natural causes at the age of 74. His wife, my grandmother, was Suessel Deutscher. She was born August 15, 1865 and died August 19 1933 at the age of 68.

Her mother, Sossie Deutscher was also born in Austrian Poland, but according to family lore, died in Palestine, then a Turkish province. I know nothing of her husband or of their life.

All of these small towns with the unpronounceable names were located in Galicia.

At the end of the eighteenth century, Poland was divided into three parts- Russian Poland (which included Warsaw), German Poland and Austrian Poland – Galicia. Poland ceased to exist as an independent country until it was reconstituted after World War I.

Galicia was then part of the Austro-Hungarian Empire. Austria, ruled by the Hapsburg dynasty, among the oldest dynasties in Europe, dating to 1275, had accumulated an enormous empire over the centuries. When the emperor addressed the population, his pronouncements were addressed to "my peoples". Austria included Northern Italy, Slovenia, much of Croatia, Bosnia-Herzegovina, what is today the Czech Republic, Slovakia and Galicia and of course Hungary which in 1865, as a sop to Hungarian nationalism, was given the honor of sharing in the empire's name. The Emperor of Austria was also King of Hungary and thus the "double Monarchy".

In this monarchy, everybody of whatever national origin was equal, but, to paraphrase

Orwell, the Austrians were more equal than everyone else.

After World War I, out of the ashes of the Hapsburg Empire, many new states emerged. Frequently, diplomats far from the realities drew borders on the ground. One of the results of this procedure was the existence of dual citizenship, which was of great importance to us when we escaped the first time.

To complicate matters, during the upheavals following the end of World War I, the section of Galicia in question was briefly part of a short-lived Ukrainian Republic.

After World War II, the Soviet Union annexed the Eastern third of Poland and Poland annexed the Eastern third of Germany, thus in effect, moving Poland some distance westward. A neat trick. This meant that the territories in question were now part of the Soviet Union. But of course, it did not end there.

After the second Russian Revolution in 1991 and the dissolution of the Soviet Union, the section of Galicia in question became part of independent Ukraine. The names of the small towns our ancestors lived in have been changed and it is very difficult to locate them on a modern map of Ukraine.

All of my grandparents and of course my parents were orthodox Jews, and I was brought up in that manner. No one in Galicia had even heard of Reform (a German-Jewish development dating to the middle of the nineteenth century and finding its most successful expression in the United States of America).

My father went to Cheder, the Jewish school, for his religious education and to the Austrian school for his secular education. My parents spoke Yiddish, Polish and German and could communicate in Ukrainian. Of course after they had lived in the United States for a while, they also spoke and read English.

I owe my parents an apology, in fact, many apologies. I know now, that my father was highly educated in Jewish lore; in fact he occasionally conducted services at the small synagogue – called a Stuebel- which we attended in Vienna. But the parents of my friends and schoolmates were University educated and could discuss literature – Goethe and Schiller, and even Shakespeare, whereas my father was more versed in the writings of Maimonides, Rabbi Caro and other Jewish sages. And that was not what I appreciated.

My father taught me that it was not necessary to speak a language in order to be able to communicate. He was able to make himself understood with a pencil and paper as long as he could write numbers. I remember particularly an incident while we lived in Nice when he negotiated a complicated deal involving the not quite legal transportation of some watches from Italy to France. His partner in the negotiations only spoke Italian, which, at that time neither my father nor I were familiar with. Nevertheless, using hands and pencils, my father managed to make all arrangements, prices, meeting places, manner of payments, and so forth.

My father had a wonderful handwriting; his Spenserian script was beautiful and inimitable. In his youth he had been an assessor, some kind of tax official working with attorneys. This made him something of an intellectual in the eyes of the rest of the family.

My father had several brothers and sisters and I know very little about them. I know there was a brother, Mendel, who visited our apartment in Vienna once with his family, and I know that they disappeared in the Holocaust. There was a sister who remained in Halicz and took care of my father's mother. I know nothing of her fate.

One brother and two sisters went to New York when my father was a child. There was little contact, but after we had reached the United States in 1941 my father managed to find them. The brother, Willy, was a waiter in a delicatessen on the lower Eastside, the two sisters were married, and everybody lived in the Bronx. Apparently, my parents had little in common with them, and the blood ties were not enough to maintain much of a relationship. I believe that one sister's married name was Fanny Lopatin. I know nothing more about them, and I was too young and self absorbed to maintain a relationship with people my parents did not seem to be interested in.

My father was a Levi and was proud of that fact, and impressed on me what an honor it was to be a Levi. He used to explain, that Cohanim were the generals, Levi the officers, and the rest of the children of Israel other ranks.

And here comes a Historical – Religious digression:

The Patriarch Jacob had twelve sons. Joseph, who became Grand Vizier of Egypt was the second youngest, and Benjamin the youngest.

When the Jews settled in Egypt at Joseph's invitation, twelve tribes developed, one from each of the sons (actually, two from Joseph).

When they left Egypt 400 years later under the leadership of Moses, each tribe bore the emblem of one of the sons. After the revelation at Sinai, Moses' brother Aaron became the chief priest, and his descendants to this day are

Cohanim - priests- with special duties and obligations in religious life.

After Canaan was conquered, the land was divided among the tribes. However, the tribe of Levi was not given land, instead its members became the acolytes of the priesthood and were supported by donations to the priesthood and from general funds.

Today, in traditional synagogues, it is the Cohanim who recite the blessings over the congregation, and the Levis present who have the privilege of pouring water over their hands to purify them before they do so.

Furthermore, during the reading of the Torah portion – every Monday and Thursday – market days in ancient Israel – and of course on Saturday, the first portion is read by any Cohen in attendance, the second by a Levi and only after that, the privilege belongs to others present.

Because of this tradition, generally a pitcher is engraved on the gravestone of a Levi, - as it is on my father's and, I hope, will be on mine.

After the zenith of the Jewish Kingdom under David and Solomon, in the tenth century before the Common Era, the kingdom split. The tribes of Judah and Benjamin formed the Southern Kingdom, the other tribes the Northern. There were, of course, Levites and Cohanim in both kingdoms.

The tradition that says that I am a Levi was passed on from father to son, and so I pass it on to my sons. It is because of this, that my name is Moshe ben Yitzchok HaLevi.

Regretfully, women are not qualified to be priests in the tradition. I am glad that today's modern Jews accept the equality of women (which the orthodox practitioners still do not do.)

In 722 before the Common Era, the Assyrians conquered the Northern Kingdom, the population was distributed throughout Assyria, and the ten tribes that had formed the Northern Kingdom disappeared from history.

Only the tribes of Judah and Benjamin remain, together with those Levites that had lived in the Southern Kingdom and from whom we are descended.

In 586 before the Common Era, the Babylonians conquered the Southern Kingdom, destroyed the temple and moved a large portion of the population to Babylon – the first of many exiles our people endured.

But this book is not a history of the Jewish people. It is my personal story. Nevertheless, I would like to point out that for Jews events that happened thousands of years ago still have immediate significance.

And now back to my story:

I believe that my parents were engaged to be married when World War I broke out in August of 1914. My father served in the Austro-Hungarian Army. He used his writing skills to advantage and managed to work in an office where was promoted to Gefreiter – something like Lance Corporal.

In 1916 my parents were married in Maehrisch-Ostrow in Moravia, part of today's Czech republic. I remember a photograph of my father in uniform, but the photo is lost. I do have a photograph of my father dating from about that time, with a mustache – which he never wore later - looking very handsome.
I know nothing about what happened to my parents during the first World War and its aftermath. I mentioned the upheavals in Galicia, so it does not surprise me that my father would wind up in Vienna, the capital of the tiny, German speaking, remnant of the Austrian Empire. My mother's family had been in Vienna for much longer. In fact, I treasure a photograph taken in Vienna in 1906, showing my grandparents and their five

children.   My mother was sixteen at the time
and a beautiful young woman.

Bottom row: Grandmother, Ella, Herz, Grandfather;
Top row: Natan, my mother, Jacob

CHAPTER 2

I was born in Vienna on September 4, 1924.

At that time we lived in the Schulerstrasse. One of my earliest memories is going with my parents to look for a larger apartment because my mother was pregnant with my sister Susi. Susi was born on May 31, 1928 and by that time we lived in a beautiful large apartment at Loewengasse 39, IIA, in the third district of Vienna.

If you visit Vienna these days, one of the tourist sites is the Hundertwasser House built by the great artist and architect Hundertwasser. Of course it is a post World War II construction. It was built immediately next door to the building where our old apartment was located.

Let me clear up some confusion about our family names.

My father's father's name was Lerner and his wife's, my grandmother's maiden name was Auster. My mother's father name, was Zweifler and his wife, my other grandmother was named Deutscher. If you have been paying attention, dear Reader, you will wonder. Well, this is of course the place for another historical digression.

Until the end of the eighteenth century, the Age of Enlightenment, the Jews of Europe had few civil rights and lived essentially in their own communities, in ghettoes or villages called Shtetls, separate from the gentiles. They maintained their traditional Jewish names, Moshe ben Yitzchak (Moses son of Isak) for instance.

With the Enlightenment, Jews began to be emancipated. Emperor Joseph II of Austria issued an Edict of Tolerance giving Jews almost the same rights as their neighbors. The Napoleonic upheaval also established equality for Jews in France and many German states. In Russia, legal emancipation did not come until the second half of the nineteenth century.

When Jews were emancipated in the Austrian possessions there was a rush to register new names. Hence, names that dealt with the professions or the locations or characteristics of the applicant. Lerner, for instance, means student, particularly of the Talmud.

Thus the many botanical names which were deemed to be pretty, the valley of roses (Rosenthal), the green fields (Gruenfeld), the mountains of flowers (Blumenberg), etc, and the names of precious minerals, Gold, Silver, Diamond, Ruby etc. and finally, the cynical names Treu (faithful), Ehrlich (honest) Schoen (Beautiful) and so forth.

At the same time, with Emancipation, Jews had to obey the secular laws of the countries they lived in. They served in the army, as my father did, and when they married, they had to have a secular ceremony in front of a government official, in addition to the religious ceremony performed by a rabbi.

My father's parents did so. My mother's parents, like many others, did not bother. Thus, this couple who lived together for their lifetimes and who were married by a rabbi, were considered unmarried in the eyes of the Austrian law, and their children, my aunts and uncles and my mother, were considered illegitimate and took the last name of their mother, Deutscher.

I knew my maternal grandparents well. They lived in Vienna in the Sebastian Kneipp Strasse in the second district, which was very heavily populated by Jews at that time. My grandfather started out as a scribe, and later became the Viennese representative of a French fashion magazine, Le Chic Parisien. As such, he traveled around Vienna mainly by streetcar, and he had a monthly pass.

I remember one Sunday when he visited us. I desperately needed a uniform scarf for the Cub Scout meeting taking place that day, and I persuaded him to go to the Scout store to get it for me. After all, he could take the streetcar without having to pay for it. He was a good grandfather.

I remember my grandmother making a mouse for me out of a handkerchief when I was sick, and singing to me some of the Yiddish songs that still touch my heart when I hear them. She was a good grandmother.

My grandmother died quite suddenly in the summer of 1933. She was only 68 years old. I was nine years old and it was the first time that I came across human mortality.

My grandfather died in 1937. Perhaps that was just as well; he missed the dispersion and partial destruction of his family.

My grandparents are buried in the Jewish section of the Central Cemetery in Vienna. I have visited their graves several times. There was a monument for my grandmother. By the time it was appropriate to place a stone for my grandfather, the family was gone from Vienna. Years after the war, my cousin Aron from Israel, my cousin Monica from Washington, D.C. and I placed a stone for my grandfather.

These were my maternal grandparents' children:

The oldest was Jacob Deutscher. He was born in Austrian Poland in 1882. He and his wife Caroline lived in Brno, today's Czech Republic. He was the central European distributor of Le Chic Parisien, and in fact, my grandfather worked with him. He had asthma, and whenever he came to visit us in Vienna we children found it fascinating to see him use a breathing aid.

He died of natural causes before the Nazi invasion of Czechoslovakia.

He had two sons, Kurt and Paul, who were college students and often came to visit us in Vienna.

I have no information as to what happened to Caroline. Paul had become a doctor of medicine and had escaped to Hungary. A non-Jewish Hungarian woman, whom he married after the war, hid him. He then practiced medicine in Hungary under its Communist regime. He had changed his name Deutscher, which was not a name to invoke feelings of friendliness, to Donath. When emigration from Hungary was possible, he and his wife moved to Munich, and he died there of natural causes a few years ago. He had no children as far as I know.

Kurt managed to get to Palestine, served briefly in the British Army, was wounded and discharged in London. When I was in London in 1944 and 1945 as an American soldier, I spent time with him and his wife and daughter. At the time, he was a waiter at the Strand Palace Hotel. After the war, he and his family came to the United States. He stayed with my parents briefly, and then moved to Chicago. He was an insurance broker there, had a son in addition to his daughter. And of course, changed his name from Kurt Deutscher to Frank Dennis.

The next brother was Nathan. Nathan was born in 1886. He was a believing Jew and an ardent Zionist. He, his wife Clara Spindel (born 1892) and their son Arnold, who is four years younger than I am, lived in Stuttgart, Germany. When the Nazis got into power, Nathan was farsighted enough to leave immediately. The family came to Vienna and moved in with my grandparents while they were attempting to get permission to move to Palestine. They were there when my grandmother died.

This was the first time I met my cousin Arnold.

The British refused almost all applications for immigration to Palestine. Eventually my uncle Nathan and his family went to Palestine on a temporary visitor's visa as representatives of Le Chic Parisien (with a letter from uncle Jacob to that effect).

When their visa expired, they remained in Palestine as illegal immigrants and became legal only when the State of Israel was established in 1948. There they used their Hebrew names, Nissan, Haya and Aron. In the early years of the state of Israel there was a tendency for people to adopt Hebrew names, and again, Deutscher was hardly a popular name. The family adopted the name Dotan, and my cousin Aron Dotan has brought great renown to that name.

At first, they had a very hard time. Nathan was an upholsterer and found it difficult to support himself. Then his wife, Aron's mother, died.

Aron told me an incident when he was very sick at home after his mother had died and his father was left as the sole caregiver. His father sat with Aron day and night for many days and pulled him through. During that time he lost his livelihood, but Aron is convinced that his father saved his life.

Eventually, Nathan married again. Aron grew up in a very traditional and very Zionist home. Aron became a Ph.D., specializing in the Masora – the earliest Hebrew grammar. He has published many scholarly articles and books. A few years ago, he was honored with the Israel prize for a lifetime of achievements.

Of course he served as a soldier of Israel in the War of Independence in 1948 and in all subsequent wars. He married Ruth Ventura, whose father had been Grand Rabbi of Alexandria, Egypt. Ruth was born in Paris.

Dr. Aron Dotan is Professor Emeritus at Tel Aviv University and is still writing and publishing.

Ruth and Aron have three children:

Zvi Dotan, born January 4, 1956 is an attorney presently serving as a Judge on the Appellate level. He lives in Tel Aviv with his wife Tali. He has three children, Ronen born 1983, Avishaq born 1991 and Sigal born April 30, 1994. Zvi has of course served in the Israeli Army as have his children.

Chaya, born on October 30, 1960 was married to a helicopter pilot and is now married to the Director of the Ben Gurion Museum in Sde Boker in the Negev.
She has a son Teva Nisan born February 10, 1989, a daughter Perach born September 2, 1990 and a daughter Shirily born February 28, 1995.

Tamar, born November 8, 1965 lives in Tel Aviv and is a social worker.

All of Aron's three children were born in Israel, which makes them authentic Sabras. They have fulfilled their military obligations as good citizens.

My mother's younger sister was Ella Deutscher, born 1896. She was reputed to have been exceptionally beautiful, and in fact, I remember her that way. She was married to a man named Jacob Necker and then divorced him. This was a great tragedy and a scandal in those days. I know her husband's name only because I have a silver Kiddush cup engraved "Ella and Jacob Necker" with the date of my B'rith – my circumcision and entry into the covenant   -   one week after my birth, September 11, 1924, and with my initials. This present from that unfortunate couple is all I know about Ella's first husband.

Eventually, Ella married a widower with two sons. His name was Willner. He had a jewelry store in St. Poelten, a small town an hour from Vienna, and their apartment was above the store. I remember staying with them once or twice. After the Nazi take-over, they tried to make their way out of what was now Germany on a very old and decrepit vessel, the Struma. The ship was supposed to go down the Danube to the Black Sea, cross into the Mediterranean through the Bosporus and the Dardanelles, and unload its passengers in Palestine. This was a forlorn hope, since the British refused admittance to desperate refugees to the country they ruled.

The engine of the Struma was in very poor shape and the ship had to stop constantly for repairs. When it reached the Black Sea, the Turks, prompted perhaps by others, refused them passage through the straits into the Mediterranean. The ship, with its engine useless, was towed into the middle of the Black Sea and abandoned together with its several hundred passengers. It blew up with total loss of life. Whether it exploded because of its defective engine, or whether a submarine torpedoed it, and if so, one from what nationality, remains a matter of conjecture.

My mother's youngest brother's name was Herz (Hans) Deutscher.

When I was born, my mother imported a young cousin of my father's from Halicz to help out, Regina. She was probably no more than seventeen years old when she came to Vienna. Herz met her in my parent's apartment and they fell in love.

In due course, they married and had a daughter, Monica, born September 8, 1932. Uncle Herz was a dental technician, they lived in an apartment in the Kolonitzgasse, directly behind the public school I attended, and I saw them frequently. Herz had his dental laboratory in his apartment, and I loved the Bunsen burner and the smell of melting wax and all the other exciting things Uncle Herz showed me.

In November 1939, after the war had started, Uncle Herz crossed the border illegally into Belgium, and in December my Tante Regina and Monica managed to follow him in the same way. They wound up in Antwerp. There was an opportunity for my Aunt Regina and Monica to go to England, but it was not possible for Uncle Herz. He sent them on, hoping to be able to follow. He never made it.

Crossing borders was more and more difficult. We know that after the German Invasion of Belgium and the Netherlands, Herz made it into France, where he found himself in German occupied territory. He managed to cross from occupied into unoccupied France, and reached Nice in April 1941 – just a month after we had left on our journey to Spain, Portugal and the United States. He was arrested by the French, interned in a French camp, transferred by the French to their German Masters and taken to Camp Drancy. From there he was transported to Auschwitz where he was murdered.

We have actually been able to trace his route – we have the number of the train that transported him to Auschwitz. Good record keeping is very much a German trait.

My aunt Regina and Monica, who was nine years old at the time, found themselves alone in London. Regina managed to get a job as housekeeper for a widower who had three children and was quite well to do. Monica was brought up in company with those children. They lived in a nice suburb of London in a comfortable house and I visited them when I was in London as an American soldier in 1944 and 1945. Of course, none of us knew Herz's fate until after the war.

In 1947, after we were certain that Herz was dead, my aunt Regina and Monica came to the United States. By that time, we were all American citizens and thus able to help them through the maze of regulations that I will describe further when I talk about my own adventures. I picked up Tante Regina and Monica when their ship arrived. They lived in Queens until Monica grew up. She was very young – only eighteen- when she married Philip Finkel.

Tante Regina married again. Her husband, Joel Filar, was a concentration camp survivor who lost his wife in the Holocaust. He used to live in Warsaw.

Monica's husband's business moved to Maryland and so they moved to Potomac, Maryland where they still live. When Philip's lumber business failed, he retired and Monica went into real estate, where she has been quite successful.

As Tante Regina and Joel got older it was very difficult for them to be so far away and so they ultimately moved to Potomac, close to Monica.

Monica and Philip have three children:

Howard, born September 18, 1956.

Jay, born December 5, 1959.

Valerie, born July 11, 1964.

I must complete the roster of my grandparents' descendants:

My sister Susi married Joseph Cahlin, against the advice of her family. They had three children and then the marriage ended. Susi married again a man named Richard Pless, and this marriage ended as well. She died in 1967 at the age of 39, most likely from an overdose of medications.

Her three sons moved to Florida where their father lived. They are:

Michael Cahlin, born June 14, 1952, presently lives in St.Albans, Vermont with his wife Nancy.

Richard Cahlin, born November 23, 1955, lives in Coconut Grove, Florida with his wife Allison. They have two children, Brittany Susan born September 28, 1984 and Alexander Brent, born October 28, 1987.

Jimmy (Duke) Cahlin, born July 1, 1959 lives in Fort Lauderdale, Florida.

I am very close to all three of them.

And now it is my privilege to list the people who have given me joy, pride and pleasure their entire lives, my children and grandchildren:

My son, David Mark Lerner, born July 12, 1952 – the greatest day of my life. David and his lovely wife Laurie Sue live in Cheyenne, Wyoming, where he has developed an Internet business.

He and Laurie have given me two wonderful grandchildren – Steven Isaac Lerner, born January 15, 1989 and Katherine Lindsey Lerner, born August 20, 1992.

My daughter, Shereen Ann Lerner, born July 10, 1955 – the greatest day of my life. Sherry lives with her husband Robert Miller in Tempe, Arizona. Sherry has a Ph.D. in Archeology and is head of her department at Mesa Community College. Rob's Ph.D. is in Anthropology and he is a consultant to various medical institutions.

They have given me two wonderful grandchildren: Alyssa Josephine Miller, born May 18, 1985 and Benjamin Jennings Miller, born June 16, 1988.

My son, Thomas Andrew Lerner, born October 14, 1956 - the greatest day of my life. Tom and his wife Kirsten Erickson are both attorneys. Tom is partner in a mid-size firm in Seattle, Washington and Kirsten works for the National Oceanographic and Atmospheric Agency of the Federal government.

They have given me three wonderful grandchildren: Noah Abraham Erickson Lerner, born July 18, 1990, Lukas Kurin Douglas Lerner, born October 10, 1992 and Willa Antonia Lerner, born March 26, 1996.

My children's mother, Julianna Kitty Glass, was born in Vienna on July 22, 1927. Our marriage ended in 1976, but we remained friends until her untimely death on August 29, 2010.

I often think of my parents or even more of my grandparents and what they would say to having descendants spread so far and wide living in places they probably never knew existed.

In 1977 I had the good fortune to meet my second wife, Lenore Blitz Kaufman. We were married on August 4, 1985. My wife, who has done me the honor to adopt my name, was born in New York City on March 25, 1937. She was a Professor of Reading and Study Skills at Westchester Community College and retired in 2005. She has made the second half of my life, which we have shared, a constant joy.

When I met her, she had three children, and then as time went on, grandchildren came along. We have been able to merge our families seamlessly. Lenore's grandchildren (who are also mine) and my own very proudly call themselves the cousins.

These are Lenore's descendants:

Jill, married to Kerry Beraud, born March 31, 1960 and is a very successful business woman on the upper levels of corporate America. Presently she lives in Weston, Mass.

She has given us two granddaughters: Nicole Dylan born July 14, 1998 and Michelle born October 8, 2000.

Douglas Kaufman, born April 16, 1962 lives with his wife Susan in South Salem, New York. He is a House Inspector in business for himself, and Susan is a computer programmer. They have given us two grandchildren, Matthew Garin Kaufman born May 24, 1994 and Talia Rose Kaufman born March 18, 1997.

Jonathan Kaufman, born April 25, 1967. He is in real estate.

And now, finally, for those readers patient enough to have reached this point, And for those who skipped these two chapters to get to the meat of the story, I can begin.

CHAPTER 3

Again, I was born in Vienna on September 4, 1924.

Many of the amenities taken for granted today did not exist then, and yet we considered that we lived very comfortably, if not luxuriously. Of course, there was no television, Internet or cellphone. We had only one radio in the apartment. We had no car, no dishwasher, no washing machine, and no central heating.

Our apartment was three flights up and there was an elevator in the building but in order to use it you had to buy tokens from the superintendent, so we always walked up. The only time we rode the elevator, was going or returning from vacation, when we had luggage.

Similarly, the only time I rode in a car was when we went to the railroad station to go on vacation. It was my privilege to go to the taxi stand and bring a taxi to our house, feeling very grand as the sole passenger for the two or three blocks from the taxi stand to our house.

My parents knew only one couple among all their friends who owned a car.

On the other hand, there was help in the house, a maid, a cook, a laundress (who came in once a week).

In my memory, our apartment was very large. It was T-shaped. You entered a hallway with coat racks and benches so galoshes could be removed. Across the entrance door was a door to a small balcony overlooking the inner courtyard of the building. The bathroom – and that was what it was, a bathroom, not a combined toilet/bathroom, was at the end of the lower bar of the T. There was a water heater in the bathroom and taking a bath took major preparations. Needless to say, we bathed only once a week. The toilet, with a small sink, was next to the bathroom.

The upper bar of the T had three very large rooms facing the street and connected to each other with French doors. One was my parents' bedroom, next came the formal dining room, and then my father's study.

Facing my parents' bedroom with windows toward the courtyard were first, the children's room where my sister and I slept and which was large enough to hold a table where the family ate on non-formal occasions, then the maid's room and then the large kitchen.

The apartment was heated by enormous tile ovens, which my father had had built and which were located between rooms, so that one oven could heat two rooms. One of the maid's duties was to make the fires, using coke, and to keep the ovens stoked. Of course during the night, the fires went out and we woke up in very cold rooms. We would go into the kitchen where my mother would light the gas oven to take the chill off, and we would get dressed there. The winters in Vienna, on the outskirts of the Alps, can be quite cold. The windows in the apartment were double French windows with a bolster between them to keep out the draft.

The apartment had been decorated by the most famous decorator in Vienna, a man named Feuer. I know this because for many years, when we were refugees and even after we settled in the United States, my mother bemoaned her life in Vienna where she had lived like a lady in an apartment decorated by Feuer.

My father was a dealer in raw furs, in other words, furs before they went through the tanning process. He had a warehouse and office in the basement of our apartment building. In the winter, he would spend a lot of time traveling through the Carpathian Mountains of Slovakia, Hungary and Rumania. He would buy the skins of freshly killed animals from local hunters and local dealers. He dealt in what he called "noble" furs, Baum marten, Stone marten, Fitch, Lynch, different kinds of foxes and mink, but he did not disdain the occasional shipment of squirrel skins.

The skins were shipped to his warehouse in Vienna where he would sort them out according to quality as full, ¾, ½ or ¼ value.

Where did my father acquire his expertise? It is one of the many questions I never asked and wish I had.

When he was in Vienna, he would always make it a point to visit the Café Fetzer in the Second District, which was the place where fur dealers congregated. He would either find a potential customer there, or send a shipment of furs on consignment to agents he worked with in Paris, London or New York. Sometimes he travelled to Paris or London on business, but he had never crossed the Atlantic.

After we finally settled in the United States and he went back into the fur business, he was constrained by our limited finances to deal only in Persian Lamb remnants. This, he considered a major and humiliating comedown.

My father always came home for the main meal of the day at 1 P.M. In Vienna, at that time, there were five meals each day. A small breakfast when you got up, another breakfast (Gabelfruehstueck), substantial enough to be eaten with a fork (Gabel), a main meal of several courses at 1 P.M., a Jause (Coffee and Cake) at 4 P.M. and a small snack at bed time. Perhaps the fact that Austria has not accomplished much on the world stage is attributable to the lack of time between meals.

Behind my father's desk in his study there was a framed certificate showing him as a member of good standing of the Association of Fur Dealers in Vienna. He was quite proud of that.

When I was six years old I began Public School in the Kolonitzschule not far from our apartment. This was a boys' school, there was a separate building for a girls' school behind it. In those days, coeducational schools did not exist in Austria.

There was one teacher assigned to each entering class who remained with this class for the four years of public school. My teacher's name was Josef Jax, and I remember him fondly. He taught everything, from reading and writing to arithmetic, geography and history.

History, as taught in Vienna in those days, ended in 1914 before the outbreak of World War I. We were taught nothing that happened after that, nor anything at all about current affairs or the current political situation. This pattern continued also when I went to high school – the Gymnasium. We were thoroughly familiar in great detail with ancient Roman and Greek history, and above all, all the heroic exploits of Austrian heroes from the Middle Ages through the two Turkish sieges of Vienna and ending with the glorious reign of the good and kind Emperor Francis Joseph I.

School was from 8 A.M. to 1 P.M. After the main meal, my mother would take my sister and me to a neighborhood park, and of course, we also had a good deal of homework.

After the four years of public school came the great divide.

People who could afford it, which included of course most if not all Jews in Vienna, tried to get their children into a "Gymnasium", which was an eight year school at the end of which there would be a major series of tests. If you passed those, you had a certificate of "Matura", which entitled you to enter the University. You also had to serve for only one year in the Austrian Army with the status of Officer Candidate.

If you were unable to enter a "Gymnasium", be it for financial or intellectual reasons, you went to a Volksschule (Public High School,) and ended your education at fourteen. Then you entered the work force. These four-year schools were free. The Gymnasia charged varying amounts of tuition.

The Gymnasia were divided into schools that concentrated on modern languages and engineering, and schools that specialized in a more classical education.

My parents had their heart set on my becoming a physician, and so I applied to the Akademische Gymnasium. This was certainly the most prestigious of the schools and the oldest, dating from 1553. The building, which housed it dated from 1865. Of course it also had one of the highest tuitions and the most difficult admission process. The school boasts among its alumni Franz Schubert, Hugo von Hofmansthal, Johann Nestroy, and many other literary and professional figures. The curriculum provided a classical education with great emphasis on Latin and Greek.

*My class – with Professor Jasbetz and Professor
Grossman, who taught drawing and art.
I am left of center with straight black hair sticking up.*

In order to be allowed to enter this school, there
was a series of written tests – all essays - and
an oral examination before a board of three
Professors. Short answer tests or multiple-
choice tests were unknown in Vienna at that
time. I still remember the fear and trembling
before that exam. Remember, I was only 9 ½
years old when I underwent that ordeal. The
anguish as to whether my name would be on
the list of acceptances posted on the front door
of the school, was unforgettable. After weeks
of waiting, the list was posted and my name
was on it.

A friend of mine, of equally intellectual Jewish background, failed to be admitted and had to spend a year in public school before being allowed to apply again. What a disgrace! And this anxiety was inflicted on children not yet ten years old.

In the fall of 1934, I started classes at the Akademische Gymnasium. The walk to and from home was very long, and the classes were very demanding. Most of my afternoons were spent studying, and, in fact, after a while, I joined an afternoon study program run by teachers in their spare time, which was essentially a second school.

My most important teacher was Professor Lackenbacher who taught Latin five times a week, and Greek four times a week. He fulfilled the functions of a homeroom teacher and remained in that position with my class for the three and a half years I spent in that school. The system was different from the system in American High Schools. In Vienna the students remained in one classroom and the Professors moved from room to room.

Our history and geography professor was a former Army Officer named Jasbetz, with whom my parents had a particular connection because he had a Polish background and they could speak to him in Polish on their visits to the school.

One of our favorite teachers was Professor Schmidt, who taught German. He allowed the class to be relatively undisciplined and was a "softie" when it came to excuses for not having done your work. I will have much more to say about Professor Schmidt later, when I describe the events after the Anschluss- the annexation of Austria by Germany.

There was segregation of the Jewish students in the Akademische Gymnasium. This was officially not because of anti-Semitism – although Austria has always been one of the most anti-Semitic countries in Europe – but for practical reasons. We had religious instruction two hours per week, and in order to avoid shifting students between classrooms, all Jewish students were permanently assigned to class B and all non- Jewish students – overwhelmingly Roman Catholic in Austria- were in class A, thus I A and I B, II A and II B, and so forth. Of course this system only worked if half the student body was Jewish. In an Austria of 6 ½ million population of which 185,000 were Jews, and considering
the prominence of the school, this fact assumed a certain significance. I believe this also applied to other Gymnasia.

Akademische Gymnasium, 2007, with students from the school

The Professor, who came to our school twice a week for an hour of religious instruction each time, was the youngest Rabbi in Vienna, Dr. Lehman. He taught us basic Judaism, and insisted that we attend services on Saturday in one of the many synagogues in Vienna. In order to prove that we had done so, we were required to produce a "Calendar Leaf", a sheet showing that week's Torah portion, handed out to students at the end of services at the synagogues. Naturally, there was a lively trade in these documents.

In 1943, when I was an American soldier at the Military Intelligence Training Center in Camp Ritchie, Maryland, there was Professor Lehman, a soldier like me. In fact we met while assigned to peel potatoes in the camp kitchen. To me, he was Professor Lehman – there was no way I would not accord him that title regardless of the circumstances. Many years later, when we both had gotten a great deal older, we met again, and wound up having dinner at his apartment on the Westside of Manhattan.

In Vienna, all Jews were members of the Jewish Cultural Community and paid real income taxes to the community, which, in turn, maintained the synagogues, old age homes, orphanages, schools and hospitals and the Jewish section of the Central Cemetery. Membership was voluntary, but if you wanted to be married by a Rabbi, buried in the Jewish Cemetery, or have your child attend Hebrew School, you had better be a member.

There were wonderful large synagogues in Vienna – I believe only one is still in existence. And there were dozens of Stuebels, small synagogues generally formed by groups of similar background. My parents belonged to one of those, and during the high holidays, we children spent time either in the synagogue with them, or, more often, in the street outside where we could play.

My parents rented a cabana in a very large pool club in the Prater, Vienna's largest park, and in the summer when it was nice, we would all walk there – a very long walk – and spend the day. My mother would bring lunch, and of course, we were not allowed into the water for an hour after eating. Immediately after the Nazi take-over, my parents received a letter canceling our membership in the club and demanding that the cabana be emptied of our deck-chairs and other possessions without delay.

In the summers we went away for four weeks to a resort hotel, most often the Hotel Hallmeyer in Voeslau. My father would come for weekends only, even though Voeslau is practically a suburb of Vienna. One summer we spent on the Semmering in the Alps, and it rained a lot and we could breathe the good fresh Alpine air that was advertised. I remember this as a very boring summer during which I played a lot of chess.

In 1937, we went on vacation to Abbazia, Italy. Today, the city's name is Opatja and after having been part of Yugoslavia, it is now in Croatia. In any case, it is a resort on the Adriatic Sea, and I remember my excitement at seeing the ocean for the first time, and at swimming in salt water.

I have a photograph of my parents, looking very elegant in their summer clothes, standing in front of the big hotel there, and another photograph of my sister and me in that spot. Forty-five years later, Lenore and I stood in exactly the same spot and had our picture taken..........

That summer I also studied for my Bar Mitzvah and it is the summer my grandfather died. My Bar Mitzvah took place in my parent's small synagogue. American style parties were not common in Austria and we were still in mourning, so we just had coffee and cake in our apartment after the ceremony. Yet, I felt a major sense of responsibility and empowerment. From that day, until I entered the U.S. Army, I put on Tefillin (Phylacteries)

every morning and kept kosher to the extent possible, even when we were on the run and sleeping in haystacks, classrooms and railroad stations.

This was the last summer of peace for us.

CHAPTER 4

On May 20, 1938, which happened to be my mother's birthday, we left Vienna and became refugees.

Before I begin to describe our Odyssey, of course there must be another historical digression:

After the dismantlement of the Austro-Hungarian Empire, the German-speaking remnant became the Austrian Republic, with a population of fewer than seven million, nearly two million of whom lived in Vienna – a capital without an empire. 185,000 Jews lived in Austria, most of them in Vienna.

The Republic was racked by dissension between right and left, which resulted in a civil war in February 1933. I remember being made to stay home from school because there was shooting in the streets. Of course for me, that was an extra holiday, and I did not mind at all. The right won after a major siege of a Communist dominated block of apartment buildings. A benevolent, conservative but anti-Nazi dictatorship was established, led by Chancellor Engelbert Dollfuss.

In Germany, many parties of the right and left competed. Adolf Hitler's party – the National

Socialistische Deutsche Arbeiter Partei – NSDAP or Nazi party (The National Socialist German Worker's Party) promised to restore Germany to its pre-World War I glory. He would do so by eliminating the source of all the evil that had befallen Germany – the Jews. And he promised to unite all German speakers in one German Empire, the Third Reich.

The first Reich ended in Napoleonic times when the Emperor of Germany was forced to abdicate and to remain only Emperor of Austria. The Second Reich was created by Prince Bismarck when he proclaimed the King of Prussia German Emperor in 1871, and this empire ended with the defeat in World War 1. Hitler's third Reich would last ten thousand years. Or so he promised.

At that time, the population of Germany was about 60 Millions and of these there were 575,000 Jews. And these 575,000 Jews, less than one percent of the population, men, women and children, were responsible for all the problems Germany had endured.

The Jews had stabbed Germany in the back and lost World War I. They were the bloodsucking capitalists. They were the international Communists. They had to be dealt with.

In January 1933, the Nazi party was the strongest party in the Reichstag, Germany's

Parliament, but did not have the majority. Nevertheless, President Hindenburg appointed Hitler Chancellor. Once in office, he quickly made himself an absolute dictator, facilitated by Hindenburg's death. Anti-Semitic laws were quickly enacted. The first concentration camp was established in Dachau, a suburb of Munich, and Hitler's opponents, as well as many Jews were imprisoned there.

Austria was the obvious first step in bringing all German speakers home into the Reich, as the phrase went. There was considerable sympathy for the Nazis in Austria, and in July 1934 a Nazi attempt to take over the government by force began: a group of Austrian Nazis invaded the chancellery, shot and wounded Dollfuss mortally, and asked Hitler to invade. Mussolini, Dictator of Italy, was not anxious to have German troops on his border, particularly since German-speaking South Tyrol had been annexed by Italy after World War I. He sent his troops to the border. Hitler was not yet strong enough to challenge him, and thus did not invade Austria.

After Dollfuss' death he was proclaimed a martyr to Austrian Independence and Kurt von Schuschnigg became chancellor. He was, by his own admission, not a democrat and saw his primary mission to preserve Austrian Independence. The Nazi party was outlawed, but they did not disappear. They were very well organized underground, awaiting the next opportunity.

Every May 1, there was a parade led by the best students from the schools to the Stadium in the Prater with memorials to our hero Dollfuss, with flags and patriotic songs and speeches. It was a point of honor for me to participate in these festivities as one of the representatives of the Akademische Gymnasium.

By 1938 Hitler felt much stronger. He had established an alliance with Mussolini, assuring him that when he meant to bring all German speakers into the Reich, he did not include the German speakers living in Italy. In mid-February of that year, he summoned Schuschnigg to his eyrie in Berchtesgaden and demanded the surrender of Austrian sovereignty and the incorporation of Austria into the Reich. Schuschnigg returned to an Austria racked by major agitation by the (still illegal) Austrian Nazis. Schuschnigg appealed to the world for help and was studiously ignored by the Western powers.

In early March Schuschnigg proclaimed a plebiscite for Sunday, 3/13 to establish once and for all whether a majority of the population wanted to remain independent or join Hitler's Reich.

Hitler chose not to risk an adverse decision. On Friday, March 11, German troops crossed the Austrian border. The first German troops arrived in Vienna on Saturday, March 12, 1938.

Schuschnigg was arrested and spent the next seven years detained in some comfort on the outskirts of a concentration camp. After the war, he wound up teaching political science in a University in the United States. This seems to be a pattern for failed leaders. Kerensky who ruled Russia for the six months from the fall of the Czar to Lenin's October revolution also became a professor of political science in the United States.

Hitler arrived in Vienna to a triumphal reception by almost all Austrians – except for the Jews. Cardinal Innitzer, the Roman Catholic Cardinal of Austria, a predominantly Catholic country, proudly proclaimed himself a Nazi and welcomed Hitler.

On April 10 there was indeed a plebiscite, conducted under the watchful eyes of German soldiers. Jews of course, were not permitted to vote. Unsurprisingly, 99.73% of all votes cast supported the Anschluss – the official title of the attachment of Austria to Germany.

The name Austria was eradicated from the books and the country became a province of Germany under the name Ostmark.

While the situation of Jews in Germany had been bad and worsening from the moment of the Nazi take-over in 1933, the progression of anti-Jewish laws and practices took time. With the Anschluss, the Austrian Nazis taught the Germans how to treat their Jews. Overnight, all civilized laws that enable people to live together were expunged from the German vocabulary.

It is not surprising that more than one third of the worst concentration camp guards and commandants were of Austrian origin.

Schools were closed for several weeks after the Anschluss. On the day schools reopened – in mid April, I reported back to my usual classroom at the Akademische Gymnasium. All Jewish students were ordered into the great assembly hall.

Our dear and beloved Professor Schmidt, proudly wearing the golden swastika in his lapel indicating that he had been a long time Nazi Party member, even when the party was illegal, spoke to us. He explained that our status and that of our families had changed dramatically with the incorporation of Austria into Germany. No longer would we be permitted to oppress the pure and innocent German people with our Jewish tricks. We all, even the youngest amongst us, had tainted blood and had to be eliminated from the

German lands. We were certainly not entitled to be educated in a German institution of such high repute as the Akademische Gymnasium. "The Fuehrer, in his wisdom, will decide what kind of education you will receive and what your fate will be. You will be notified of his decision in due course. In the meantime, you will learn a valuable lesson about your new status."

Then the forty percent of the student body who were Jewish, were led outside the school, given toothbrushes and buckets of water, and forced to scrub the sidewalks around the school, the sidewalks, which, according to Professor Schmidt, we had polluted for too many years.

The Director of the School, Dr. Marcus, who happened to be Jewish, and several Jewish professors, were made to scrub the sidewalks with us.

Some of our former classmates, clad in Hitler Jugend uniforms, stood guard over us and made sure we scrubbed enthusiastically. Several policemen kept order as there was a large throng of by-standers watching us and enjoying the spectacle.

It was cold in early April, although the sun was shining. I was still too young to wear long trousers. I wore shorts and long, over the knee, stockings. As I moved on my knees on the rough sidewalk, scrubbing as ordered, the stockings tore, and soon my knees were bloody. The knuckles of my hand holding the toothbrush were scratched by the sidewalk, and my hands soon were frozen. I began to envy the seventh and eighth graders who wore long pants.

We had been ordered to pile our backpacks in a corner of the building. When we were finally released and permitted to go home, I had trouble finding mine with my stiff and frozen hands.

When I reached home, my parents were horrified. Neither my sister nor I went to school again in Vienna.

I do not know whether this event was the final trigger that prompted my parents to leave. In fact, to my great regret, I never bothered to ask my parents what made them decide so quickly to abandon everything in order to save our lives.

There were other demonstrations that we were now being treated as lepers, without rights, and that all our neighbors saw it as their mandate to eliminate us from the city and country we had believed was ours.

I had been an active and enthusiastic cub scout looking forward to being promoted to the Boy

Scouts on my fourteenth birthday. I had the honor of carrying my troop's flag when we were marching along to an outing. The flag was kept in our apartment. Within days of the Anschluss, the Boy Scouts had been absorbed into the Hitler Youth. Two of my former friends, proudly wearing the Hitler Jugend uniforms, came to our apartment and demanded the flag. They acted as if we contaminated them by our mere presence in our own home.

Considering all the terrible things that happened to Jews, this was certainly a minor incident, but I was thirteen and this rankled far beyond its significance.

Foolishly, I went to the neighborhood barbershop where my father and I had gone for many years, to get a haircut. I sat there for two hours being ignored with everyone else getting his turn, until my father came to pick me up.

The superintendent of our apartment building, a man named Maresch, came to my father and said to him: " This is an opportunity – you turn over your business to me, that way it will be owned by an Aryan, and you continue to run it and we will allocate the profits properly." Wisely, my father told him that he needed to think about it.

One time, in the middle of the night, my parents woke my sister and me and hurried us out of the apartment in our pajamas, just with overcoats. We spent the rest of the night in the apartment of friends close by. Apparently, someone had telephoned and told my parents that the Gestapo was on the way to arrest us.

What other incidents happened, and what happened to friends of my parents, I do not know, - my parents made every effort to shield us. There was enough, however, for them to make the decision to leave.

Look at the situation: My father was 49 years old, my mother 48; I was 13 ½ and my sister 9. My father was an established and respected businessman, with bank accounts, stocks of merchandise in his warehouse, accounts receivable, and a lovely home. My mother had lived like a lady, in an apartment decorated by Feuer, with household help, friends and relatives around her.

I can never praise enough and appreciate enough the courage that it took for my parents to abandon everything they had worked for all their lives, and to go into the unknown.

Had they not done so, I would not be here to write this memoir. There is not a shadow of a doubt that their decision to leave saved our lives.

How many Jews died because they clung to their possessions and planned to leave only after transferring their belongings and their funds? How many never made it out?

I emphasize this, because this is a cautionary tale, and I want all of you who read this to remember that life comes first. When my parents made their decision, there had not yet been a Holocaust. Who, in fact, could imagine that a civilized nation could create camps designed to murder an entire people?

Today, now that we know that Auschwitz actually existed, it is easier to believe that it can happen again.

So remember my parent's decision, and teach it to your children – first save your lives, and never mind possessions.

Just before the Anschluss my father had made a shipment of squirrel skins to his agent in London – a distant cousin named Josef Markiewicz – and the value of that shipment represented the totality of the funds he had outside the country. Everything else had to be abandoned.

My father went to the consular section of the Czechoslovak Embassy and persuaded them that Halicz, his birthplace, was a suburb of

Presov in Slovakia. He thus obtained four valid Czechoslovak passports for the four of us.

We packed one suitcase apiece. It is odd what one takes along, and what one leaves behind in such a situation. For me, what was important were my books of Schiller, my Schliegel and Tieck translation of Shakespeare – I had read all of Shakespeare in German long before understanding much of it – and my Goethe. But Goethe has written too much, and the many volumes of his writings had to be abandoned.

Did my parents know, when we left, that it was forever? I do not know. Perhaps they thought that the situation would stabilize, that the world would speak out on behalf of the Jews of Germany and Austria, and that we would be able to return. Even if they held such a forlorn hope, it does not detract from their courage.

On Friday, May 20, 1938 – even though it was Shabbat, even though it was my mother's birthday, we took the overnight train to Paris.

I remember, in the middle of the night, when we were about to cross the border into France, the German customs inspector asked my father: "Are you coming back?" and I remember my father's answer: "Freilich." (Certainly).

It was not an expression he normally used.

In the morning, on Saturday, May 21, 1938, we arrived in Paris and our Odyssey began.

CHAPTER 5

My father negotiated for a room in a small hotel, the Hotel Paris-Rome, 4 Rue de Provence. This small hotel, remarkably, still exists today. There we had one room for the four of us. The Patron, a huge man in an undershirt, slept the days away in an alcove off the entrance, and always seemed annoyed when someone needed him or checked in or out.

We were among the first refugees who had succeeded in escaping from Vienna, and thus were able to obtain French residence permits and identity cards, which of course prohibited us from any gainful employment. These "Cartes d'Identite Non-Travailleur" were crucial documents during our entire stay in France, and had to be extended periodically at the local gendarmerie.

In the lobby of the hotel I met a boy a couple of years older than me. His family consisted of Jews who had escaped Hitler's Germany and had moved to Barcelona, Spain. When the fighting in the Spanish Civil War reached Barcelona, they escaped again, this time to Paris. My new friend had learned Spanish in Barcelona, and I watched him communicate with the Patron in broken French based on his knowledge of Spanish, and with elaborate gestures. This was an inspiration for me.

My father and I had a conversation about languages; we felt that it was unfortunate, given the circumstances, that I had studied Latin and Greek, instead of French and English. In any case my father assigned me the task of learning both of these languages quickly, so that I could interpret for the family. Fortunately, I discovered that I had a reasonable facility in picking up languages,. My studies of Latin and Greek, both of which were the foundation of modern European languages, were very helpful.

First, it was necessary for my father to go to London and to sell the shipment of squirrel skins on consignment with his agent, so that we could have some cash. He took me along and placed me in a boarding school in Brighton for four weeks for the sole purpose of learning English.

I was completely miserable. It was the first time that I had been away from the family, and I had no way of communicating with anyone. But it was there that I learned to read English books and at least understand some spoken English, but my ability to speak was very limited. After four weeks my father picked me up. We spent a day or two in London, and then returned to Paris.

It was now the summer of 1938. My parents were busy, and my mother kept my sister with her. The fur market, at that time, was in the Rue du Faubourg Poissoniere, where the dealers were and where the action took place in the streets and cafes. My father spent his days there trying to do some business, and my mother and sister often were there with him. The fur trade was Jewish, and thus the market was a source of information as to what was going on in the world we had left.

I spent my days alone – mostly wandering about Paris. We had come to Paris not as tourists but as refugees, so we never did any sight seeing as a family, and I knew nothing about that beautiful and historic city. But I learned about Paris very quickly. It is a wonderful city for walking – there are new and fascinating views around every corner.

The streets of Paris are named after the great men and women of French history or about the locations of great events, and the origin of the street names is listed on the street signs. So in deciphering these signs I not only improved my sketchy knowledge of French, I learned French history.

I was alone most of the time, depending on myself for entertainment, and the only entertainment available to me was reading books. I was lost without access to libraries and books. I haunted the second hand bookstores for books in German, but they were extremely rare. So I began to read books in French and in English wherever I could lay my hands on them.

There were two large bookstores on the boulevard not far from our hotel, and I would frequently steal books there, read them and return them – or rather exchange then for others. By returning the books I felt that I had committed no crime.

Once, during my walks, I discovered the Louvre. I had no idea that such a place existed, but stumbled on it inadvertently. I found out that entrance to the Museum was free of charge – in those days. I ran all the way home and forced my family to follow me immediately to this magnificent new discovery. The distance between the Louvre and the Rue de Provence is considerable, and after following me all the way there, my family was less than enthusiastic about my discovery. However, the Museum became one of my favorite destinations, and I could explore it at leisure. In those days they were few people in Museums. Today's throngs absorbing culture were far in the future.

On one of my walks, I came to the beautiful Place de la Concorde, and saw the American Embassy on one of its corners. I walked into the consulate in the rear, and came home with four application forms for an American Immigration Visa. When I presented these to my parents, they were not very interested. They felt certain that with the growing worldwide opposition to Nazism and revulsion against its racial attitudes, Hitler's government would not last, and we could return to a safer Austria. If worse comes to worst, we could settle in Paris, where there was a large Jewish community, and my father had many business contacts.

Besides, the difficulty of getting an Immigration Visa to the United States was enormous. First, you had to get a quota number based on your place of birth, and there were few quota numbers available for Central Europeans. Then, when your quota number finally came up, you had to show an "Affidavit of Support". This was a document, sworn to by an American citizen resident in the United States that guaranteed that the potential immigrant would never become a public charge, but that in the event that he could not support himself, the guarantor would support him. A recent income tax return had to be attached to the affidavit to demonstrate the guarantor's ability to perform this undertaking.

Where would we find such a guarantor in the United States? In any case, the question was academic. At the time I obtained the applications, our quota number based on my father's place of birth, would entitle us to apply for a visa five years in the future.

To me, America sounded wonderful. Of course I was steeped in the Wild West stories of James Fenimore Cooper and Karl May, but even without them, the United States was the land of infinite possibilities. It was the country where most of the movies I loved were made, and it was new – not hidebound like old Europe. So I nagged and pleaded and got my parents to fill out the applications, and carried them personally to the American Consulate. It was, as I pointed out to my parents incessantly, another option and it is always good to have options.

By the end of the summer, we moved to another hotel – the Hotel Montyon in the Rue de Montyon, where we had two connecting rooms and a hot plate. The hotel was not far from the Folies Bergere Theater, and I managed to improve my knowledge of human anatomy by studying the photographs of the topless dancers advertising the shows.

When the school year started, early in September of 1938, I entered the Ecole de Commerce, 39 Avenue Trudaine, a regular French High School, and my sister Susi entered a public school. I sat in the classroom day after day listening to lectures in French. One day, miraculously, I began to understand what the teacher was saying, and before you know it, I was reasonably fluent in French and could actually read and write grammatically correct sentences. I am certain that I absorbed French by osmosis, through my pores, so to speak, but that my studies of Latin and Greek under Professor Lackenbacher helped me enormously.

Early in my attendance in the school, a fellow student called me "Sale Juif" (Dirty Jew). I remembered what I had had to listen to in Vienna, but also that we were now in a country that would not support this kind of behavior. So I jumped him. The more distant my memory is from the actual event, the bigger he grows in my mind. In any case, I fought this giant thirteen year old, until a teacher separated us. I must have inflicted enough pain on him, while absorbing a lot myself, that I was never called names again in this school.

In the summer of 1938 the "free world" led by the United States, had organized a conference in Evian, France, on the shores of lake Geneva. The conference was supposed to solve the problem of the Jews no longer able to live in Germany. Out of the 575,000 Jews who lived there on the accession of Hitler, nearly half had left by that time, so the conference had to deal with 300,000 German Jews and 185,000 Austrian Jews. The conference was a complete failure. None of the attendees were willing to allow a handful of Jews to enter their countries beyond their normal immigration procedures.

This encouraged the Germans and validated their belief that they had to get rid of their Jews in any way they wished, and that no one in the world would object. It led the way inevitably to their "final solution."

In September of 1938, there was another crisis orchestrated by the Germans. Keeping his promise to unify all German speakers under his flag, Hitler demanded that the ethnic Germans living in the border region of Czechoslovakia, called the Sudetenland, be joined to the German Reich. He was strong enough then, to threaten war if his demands were not granted.

There was a conference in Munich, attended by Hitler, his now ally Mussolini of Italy, French President Edouard Daladier, and British Prime Minister Neville Chamberlain. No representatives of Czechoslovakia were invited to attend.

Hitler got what he wanted. The German speaking section of Czechoslovakia was annexed by Germany. As a bonus, Hitler got the Skoda armament works, which were located in these territories. Hitler promised that he had no further territorial ambitions in Europe. Chamberlain returned to England waiving the treaty and saying that he got "peace in our time". How wrong he was became evident very soon. Munich has become a synonym for appeasement ever since then.

After Hitler's triumph in Munich, this was the next step. For more than 120 years, until after World War I, Poland had been divided into Russian, German and Austrian Poland, Many people had moved from the Polish provinces into the cities of Germany and Austria, among them many Jews.

Hitler decided that all Jews born in reconstituted and independent Poland and residents of Germany (including Austria) were not German citizens and should be expelled to Poland. Many thousands of families were rounded up and forcibly brought to the Polish border. It was November, cold and rainy, and the people were left in an open field without shelter. The Polish government decided not to allow these people into their country; they considered them German citizens and not Polish. For many days there was tremendous suffering from the elements, until the Western powers were able to persuade the Polish authorities to admit these people.

A seventeen-year-old boy, the son of a family placed in this untenable position, became outraged about this. His name was Herschel

Grynszpan. He was visiting relatives in Paris. He was able to acquire a gun, walked into the German Embassy and shot and killed the first German he saw, a minor consular official named Von Rath.

This was the pretext for "Kristallnacht" – the night of broken glass – in Germany. Encouraged and organized by the German government, mobs rampaged through the country, burning and destroying synagogues, Jewish owned homes and businesses, and beating any Jews they could find. Many Jews were arrested and taken to concentration camps. The flood of refugees increased.

At that point we all realized that there would be no return to Vienna as long as Hitler was in power. In spite of Chamberlain's assurance that the Munich treaty would ensure "peace in our time", we began to be more and more certain that there would be another war.

Of course we were safe and secure in Paris. In World War I, the Germans could not take Paris. This time, we were protected by the Maginot Line, a series of fortresses with fixed guns facing Germany from the Swiss to the Belgian border. This line, build by French Defense Minister Maginot, could never be breached.

Of course, in World War I, the Germans went through neutral Belgium to attack France's undefended north, but they wouldn't do that again?

Besides, France had the largest Army in Europe, and more troops in its colonies.

Nevertheless, we began to understand that it would be better if we left Europe, if we ever wanted to have a normal life again. Obtaining the American visa was hopeless; we did not have five years to wait for the quota number. We applied to the British for permission to go to the British Mandate of Palestine, but there again the number of admission permits was over-subscribed for many years in the future. We applied to Australia through an immigration lawyer in Canberra, and to Canada through an immigration lawyer in Ottawa. After months of correspondence, both countries turned us down because we were "not of the right ethnic stock." Those were the words in both rejection letters- they were the same. It is hard to imagine this today, or is it?

In the spring of 1939, in violation of all treaties, the Germans moved into what used to be Czechoslovakia. They occupied the Czech part, Bohemia and Moravia, and called it a protectorate, with a German Governor. Slovakia was made into an independent country, of course a client state of Germany. The persecution of Jews in former Czechoslovakia began in full force.

At that point, even the most fervent appeasers in the West began to realize that war was inevitable, and even Prime Minister Chamberlain finally began to rearm.

In the summer of 1939, we moved to Nice. My father had developed some business that required him to be near the Italian border. He found us a furnished apartment at 12 Rue Dalpozzo. For the first time in more than a year, we had a living room, bedrooms and a kitchen. By that time, although I was only 14 ½, I participated fully in the family councils, and of course, because of my language skills, assisted in the execution of our plans. Our move was prompted not only by my father's business ventures, but we assumed that Paris would be bombed once war broke out, and we hoped – against hope- that Italy would remain neutral.

This may be the time for a digression on morality and survival.

During the three years we spent in France, we lived in a twilight area between totally law-abiding citizens and total criminals. We violated the law in many ways – we dealt in the black market, in illegal currencies, later, when rationing came into effect, in ration cards and foods, and of course in all kinds of government permits and unauthentic documents. We participated in smuggling ventures, and above all, we worked, in spite of the fact that our residence permits prohibited us from doing so. As a youngster, I was able to go places and do things that adults could not do. I was a courier, a messenger, and a full participant in all our actions.

I make no apologies, and I will not go into further details. But I quote from the Brecht/Weil "Three-Penny Opera": " First feed the face then talk morality."

Life in Nice, at the beginning was almost normal. We made friends- I was particularly friendly with a German Jewish refugee named Juli Hammerslag, who eventually wound up in Canada, and with three brothers named Bleiweiss. I do not know whether they survived, I can only hope so.. These kids were more or less my age, and had had similar experiences, and we would pal around. The beach was only a block from our apartment, and I even acquired a second hand bike, which was very useful for some of my black market activities.

The French Riviera was probably more beautiful then than it is now, because it was not overrun by tourists and high-rises. I rode my bike from Monte Carlo to Antibes and Cannes, and to the hill villages like Grasse and St. Paul de Vence. This is one of the loveliest areas in the world. The terrain is very mountainous, but I had a lot more energy then, than I have now, and the views were always exhilarating.

For my second year in a French School, I entered the Ecole de Commerce et Hoteliere on the Rue de France. By now my French was fully fluent, and I could compete on even terms with all the other students.

And then the war started.

CHAPTER 6

On August 23, 1939 the world was stunned by the news that Hitler and Stalin, the Dictator of Soviet Russia, who had been the worst of enemies, had signed a non-aggression pact. Only later, did we find out that this pact included another division of Poland.

For some time Hitler had demanded that Danzig be joined to Germany. This was part of his promise to bring all Germans into the Reich. Danzig had been declared an independent city. It was inhabited by a majority of Germans but had a very large minority of Poles. It was separated from Germany by what was called the Polish corridor, a small strip of land with the city of Gdynia, Poland's only connection to the Baltic ocean.

Hitler demanded not only Danzig, but the Polish corridor. Surrendering this would have left Poland without any outlet to the sea, and Poland refused.

And then came the Stalin- Hitler Treaty (better known as the Ribbentrop/Molotov pact, after the foreign ministers who negotiated it.)

On September 1, 1939 Germany attacked Poland with all her forces, caused immeasurably damage to Warsaw with vicious bombing attacks and advanced into Poland on all fronts. Britain and France finally realized the hopelessness of appeasement, and declared war.

World War II had begun.

The Soviet Union advanced into Poland from the East, and occupied one third of Poland as agreed in the treaty, and Germany occupied the rest.

Poland again ceased to exist.

Out of a population of over 33 million, ten percent, more than three million were Jews.

Poland had been the center of gravity of European Jewry. Jews had lived in Poland for over a thousand years. In Warsaw one third of the city's population of one and a half million were Jews. There was a rich intellectual life throughout Poland, with schools, academies, newspapers and books, theaters and concerts. There were old age homes, orphanages, hospitals and many, many synagogues.

All of these people now found themselves at the mercy of the Nazis.

For us, in the West, nothing happened.

After the defeat of Poland, nothing happened. The Germans seemed to be busy absorbing their new conquest, and Britain and France, having declared war, seemed to feel that they did not have to do anything else.

The French sat behind their-to them-invincible Maginot line. And nothing happened.

The British finally began to take the war seriously. Winston Churchill was called out of the political wilderness, where he had warned against Hitler for many years, to become Lord of the Admiralty, but Prime Minister Chamberlain, the architect of the Munich surrender, still remained in office. An expeditionary force was sent to France, to help the French Army sit behind the Maginot line. And so they all sat. And nothing happened.

Occasionally, there would be a communiqué from the front about a dogfight in the air, or an exchange of artillery in one sector.

After a while this period got a name: in French "drole de guerre" (funny war), in English it was called the phony war.

I went to school in Nice and life continued.

There was some rationing, which enabled us to do a little business in various coupons.

We expected Italy to enter the war on the side of Germany, and were fully prepared to leave vulnerable Nice the moment that happened, and return to Paris, but Italy remained neutral.

Our various applications to emigrate were turned down. We expected to remain in France until inevitably, the Allies would beat Germany as they had done in World War I. After all, who could stand against the might of the British and French Empires, which, with their colonies, outnumbered the Germans manifold?

Whether we would then return to Vienna or remain in France was never discussed.

In April 1940 Germany occupied Denmark in one day without resistance, and in a few days occupied Norway. Denmark was a major food producer, and Norway's fjords were a wonderful resource for German U-Boats.

Still nothing else happened. The phony war continued.

On May 10, Germany advanced on all fronts and in a lightning strike occupied Luxembourg, the Netherlands and Belgium, entered France across the Belgian border where the Maginot Line did not extend, broke through French defenses and defeated the French in the first of many tank battles of the war.

Chamberlain finally resigned and Winston Churchill became Prime Minister.

The British Expeditionary Force was trapped along the sea near Dunkirk. The men of that force were saved in a heroic undertaking by British civilians sailing their own small boats, and by the British Navy. All their equipment was lost.

On June 10, 1940 Italy finally declared war on the side of Germany.

Now, we made our worst mistake of that time.

CHAPTER 7

There were no fortifications to protect Nice against Italy. After all, in World War I Italy had fought against Germany on the side of the allies. We were convinced that Italy would occupy Nice very quickly. We were equally convinced that the French would stop the Germans from entering Paris. That is precisely what they had done in World War I.

It is said that generals always fight the last war. We were lay people. Can we be blamed for doing the same?

So we packed our bags and took the overnight train to Paris. The train took much longer than the schedule showed. Other more important trains constantly sidetracked it – military trains no doubt. A ten-hour trip took nearly twenty-four hours.

We arrived in Paris on June 12. The Railroad Station was overwhelmingly crowded. People clamored for tickets to go anywhere away from Paris.

We found out that the French Army had been defeated, that Paris had been declared an open city, and that the German Army was expected to enter Paris momentarily.

We did not even leave the railroad station. The French government had relocated to Bordeaux, and we decided to follow them.

It is remarkable that in the midst of such chaos, the French transportation system attempted to continue as if nothing had happened. We got on a train to Bordeaux.

But indeed, something had happened. A few miles outside of Paris, the German Air Force had destroyed the railroad tracks. We left the train- there were thousands and thousands of us – and started to walk along the tracks. Rumor had it that another train would be waiting a few miles down the road where the tracks were working.

Two or three times German planes buzzed the mass of humanity walking along the tracks. Every time, people panicked and many threw themselves into the ditches along the tracks. I did not see any planes firing, but word spread that they had strafed a column of fleeing Parisians at another location.

After several hours of very slow progress, we came indeed to a station where we were told a train would arrive from the West and would load and take us to our destination. We waited for hours, without food and water and with the very limited facilities offered by this small station. Eventually a train did arrive. It was instantly occupied by the mass of people, with many sitting on the roofs of the wagons, on bumpers and between cars.

Eventually, with many stops and delays, we arrived in Bordeaux.

We left the station and found a café nearby to get some food and discuss our next move.

A German motorized column drove right past us.

Obviously, Bordeaux was not a good choice.

There was a bus stop near the station, and busses were still going. We found a bus going south toward the Spanish border.

Many hours later, we arrived in St. Jean de Luz.

St. Jean de Luz, Bayonne and Biarritz were famous French resorts on the Atlantic Coast, just north of Spain. In the nineteenth and early twentieth century, Biarritz particularly was a high fashion venue. As a result, there were lots of hotels in the area.

We found a room in a small hotel near the railroad station, and for the first time in four days slept in beds.

Now King Rumor ruled. No one knew how far the German advance would proceed and how much time we had until we were overrun by German troops.

After the defeat of Poland some Polish troops had been transported to France by the British fleet, so that they could continue to fight. There was a story making the rounds that they had been seen near the port, and that the British Fleet would again rescue them. Rumor also had it, that the British would also rescue those refugees who were in greatest danger from the Germans, namely Jews. Some people believed this so fervently, that hundreds sat on their suitcases in the harbor, waiting for British rescuers.

We did not have any illusions about British altruism, particularly as far as Jewish refugees were concerned.

Rumor also had it that there was a Spanish consul in a hotel in Bayonne who would issue visas to Spain. Spain was an ally of Germany, under the leadership of Francisco Franco, who had won the civil war with Germany's help. But Spain was neutral, and if we could get there, perhaps we would be safe from the Germans.

By that time, the French transportation system had finally been reduced to shambles. My father and I hitchhiked to Bayonne, leaving my mother and sister to rest in St. Jean de Luz. We found the hotel where the Spanish consul indeed issued visas. Thousands of people surrounded the place and it seemed impossible to get in.

After some hours of waiting around, my father got nervous about being separated from my mother and sister, and about the problem of hitch-hiking back. He felt that there was no chance to get into the hotel to see the consul.
By that time, I had made friends with a young woman, my age, who apparently worked or lived in the hotel. I insisted that my father give me our passports, and promised him that I would get back to St. Jean de Luz within a few hours one way or another.

My new friend sneaked me into the hotel through a back door. I got to the suite where the Spaniards were working. There was a large conference table, and ten or twelve clerks were sitting around it with piles of passports in front of them, into which they placed the all-important stamp.

There was an advantage to being less than sixteen years old, whereas an adult would have been noticed; nobody paid attention to a kid. I took our four passports and slid them on a pile being worked on by one of the clerks. I watched as he stamped the visas into each of them. I watched as our passports were delivered to the head of the table where the consul affixed his signature.

And I watched as he crossed out the visas and returned the passports. I was told that Czechoslovakia did not exist any more, and that therefore our passports were invalid.

It broke my heart.

I still have these passports and you can see the crossed out visas in each of them.

There was nothing further to be done. I started on the way back to St. Jean de Luz – it was only 15/20 kilometers, I believe- and I got a ride fairly quickly.

Czech Passport

Czech Passport crossed out by Spanish consul.

As we were driving along the Corniche, a highway well above the seashore, we had a clear view of several British warships being attacked by a number of German planes and returning anti-aircraft fire.

It was night – the view of the sea below us, the exploding shells like fireworks, the planes circling and dropping bombs presented an unforgettable spectacle. The man who had given me a ride stopped his car, and we sat for a long time in perfect safety – we thought – watching the reality of war.

Eventually, the attacks ceased. Whether there was any damage to the British ships I do not know, nor did I see any German planes shot down.

I returned to my family in St. Jean de Luz very late. They were of course worried about me. And then I had to disappoint them by showing them our passports with the Spanish visas crossed out.

This ended our hopes to escape into Spain. There was a possibility of crossing the Pyrenees on foot, and we considered it briefly, but we decided against it, partly out of fear that my mother and sister were incapable of the hardships of such a trip, and partly because we were certain to be interned by the Spaniards, who, after all, were allies of Hitler.

By June 21, France had surrendered. The French government did so in spite of the fact that they still had the colonies with a large part of the French Army and they still had the French Navy. What they did not have is the indomitable will of a Winston Churchill.

A new French government was formed. Marshall Petain, who had been a hero in World War I, a man well over eighty and perhaps somewhat senile, was resurrected and named Chef d'Etat – Chief of the State – instead of President. Pierre Laval, an anti-Semitic ultra right-wing supporter of Germany from way back, became Prime Minister.

The armistice between this German-appointed government and Germany called for the entire Northern half of France, including Paris, and the entire Atlantic Coast to be occupied by German troops. The rest of France was called the Free Zone (Zone libre) and was governed by Petain and Laval. The seat of the new French government was to be Vichy, a resort town in central France near the demarcation line between occupied and "free" France, which had the advantage of having many hotels which could be used for the offices and residences of the bureaucrats of the new French government.

To their eternal shame, the colonies of the French Empire and the French Navy submitted to the dictates of the Vichy government and ceased fighting the Germans. Only one man, an obscure brigadier general named Charles de Gaulle, escaped to Britain and formed a French Government in exile. Unelected by his countrymen, and unaccepted by the Allies, he maintained that he alone represented a France that would not bow to the German conquerors.

When the news of the details of the Armistice agreement became public, we knew that we could not stay in St. Jean de Luz, which was due to be occupied by German troops   We found a truck, which took us and many others a couple of hours to the East, to the first town that, according to the map, would be in the zone libre.

That town was Pau. Pau was filled to overflowing with refugees from all over France attempting to escape from the zone to be occupied by Germany. Pau was a small town with a shortage of housing. The Mayor opened the schools and we found ourselves settling into a classroom for the night, together with many other people.

A young man, a teacher at that school, picked the four of us and took us to his apartment where he lived with his mother. For the next few days, we slept on couches and on the floor of his apartment. This was many times better than sleeping in a classroom. This young man, by his unselfish action, restored our faith in the goodness of people.

A word about France and the French:

I love France. France is one of the most beautiful countries in the world. I love French culture, literature and the arts. I love the French language. I can still recite passages from Corneille, Racine, Rostand and others, that can bring tears to my eyes.

But the French can be the most xenophobic people in the world. They can be incredibly selfish, hypocritical and anti-Semitic.

They can also be noble, self-sacrificing and brave.

France is the country of the absolutist Bourbon kings – and the country of Voltaire and Rousseau.

France is the country that gave us the Declaration of the Rights of Man -and the Terror.

France gave us the Napoleonic Wars, which killed many, many people – but spread the ideals of equality and opportunity throughout the world.

France is responsible for the Dreyfus Affair, where an innocent man was sent to Devil's Island by a conspiracy of the entire French General Staff, because he was Jewish. And France gave us Emile Zola who defended him.

It was the French police, who, under German orders, rounded up all the Jews in occupied Paris, kept them imprisoned in the Vel d'Hiver and loaded them into trains to Auschwitz.

It was the French, in occupied France, who created camps for stateless Jews from which, among many others, my Uncle Herz was sent to be murdered.

It was the French who collaborated with their German conquerors against their former Allies.

But it was also the French, who formed resistance cells against the Germans.

My feeling about the French, as you can see, is very ambivalent.

I have met good and bad French people – and I guess that says it all. They are human, with all the faults and virtues of common humanity.

The teacher in Pau behaved nobly toward us. What happened to him and to his family, and how he behaved toward others, I cannot tell.

There was no point in staying in Pau. We found a trucker who promised, for a steep fee, to take us to Marseilles. This was another mistake. A number of other refugees joined us on the truck. We found that we had fallen into the hands of crooks.

The trucker, his partner and his girlfriend claimed that they had no gasoline. We spent nearly a week crossing from Pau to Marseilles – a trip that should have taken less than a day. We spent the nights in haystacks and barns, the days in villages where the trucker disappeared, ostensibly hunting for gasoline and constantly demanded more money. By the time we finally arrived in Marseilles, my mother's fur coat had disappeared from her suitcase, but we were glad to have escaped from these criminals' clutches.

We spent a week or two in a small hotel in Marseilles assessing the situation. While this was the major port in unoccupied France, there did not appear any place to go. The trains were running again. We still had the apartment in Nice and Italy had made no move to invade France. So we returned to Nice.

We had been on the road for six weeks, suffered a great deal, lost a lot of money and my mother's fur coat, and all for naught.

CHAPTER 8

Charles de Gaulle broadcast a speech from London. He said that France had lost a battle, but France had not lost the war. He exhorted the French to fight on.

Few French followed him, and the French colonies continued to obey what became known as the Vichy government.

The bulk of the French Fleet retreated to the harbor of Mers el Kebir, near Oran, Morocco. The Armistice agreement had specified that the French Fleet would not be turned over to the Germans, but the British, with good reason, distrusted any agreement Germany made. On July 3, 1940 British forces attacked and destroyed the bulk of the French Fleet. Over 1200 French sailors lost their lives, and of course this helped to turn French sentiment away from Britain toward a more cooperative attitude with Germany.

For all intents and purposes, France changed from a German adversary to a German puppet, with its industry in the service of the German war machine. It would be a long time before de Gaulle's unelected government in exile had any impact on life in occupied and unoccupied France.

The Petain/Laval government passed a number of anti-Semitic laws which were actually harsher than the laws in Germany. Rationing, which had been moderate before the defeat, became much more severe, and enforcement even more so. We did not dare in these new circumstances to play the games with ration coupons we had played before.

Each family was assigned to one particular grocery where we were allowed to shop with the coupons we had, but the grocery to which we were assigned exhibited the worst traits of French xenophobia and anti-Semitism, and we only got the worst of what was left over.

There was constant anti-Semitic propaganda. The government organized a youth movement on the Hitler-Youth model. It was called the Milice. At first it formed para-military units helping the government keep order. Eventually they formed combat units on the Russian front – more cannon fodder for Germany.

Milice headquarters was in the rue Dalpozzo, two houses from where we lived, and of course, they knew who we were.

Once, as I came home, a bunch of them threw a paper bag filled with ink at me. I was covered with ink to their great amusement. But this was the worst direct incident I was involved in at that time.

Those of you who know the words of the French national anthem, the Marseillaise, will appreciate the dilemma of the Vichy government. You cannot remove the Marseillaise from France, but in the circumstances the first six stanzas were politically incorrect. After all, they rouse the people to fight against the invaders who come to murder them and their families.

The solution was to make the seventh stanza the official anthem of Vichy France. It speaks of youth with hopes for a better future.

CHAPTER 9

Our situation seemed very precarious. The new French laws against Jews placed us in imminent danger. With the Italian/French border closed, my father's business ventures came to a stand still, and our black market games became much too dangerous. In addition to all other problems, we had to face the fact that we could run out of money.

My sixteenth birthday came and went and we saw no way forward. When school started in September 1940, I resumed going to classes, but with little interest. We had no idea how long we could stay in what was becoming a more and more dangerous situation, nor where we could go.

My parents found another method to increase our funds. Every evening they went to the casino and watched for someone who appeared to be winning big. They then followed his lead and bet in the same manner. Apparently, this system worked and they did all right, but many a time I remember their coming home late at night arguing that they had picked the wrong gambler, or that they had not stopped soon enough.

One day, I happened to be walking past the United States Consulate, which at that time was on the Avenue Victor Hugo not far from our apartment. Just as a matter of curiosity, I went in and asked about the status of our applications. The young man who was vice-consul promised to check with the Embassy in Paris. Remember, this was well over a year before Pearl Harbor and the United States was still neutral.

A few weeks later, the consul informed us that our quota number had been reached. The five-year period we had been told about two and a half years earlier had shrunk. Obviously, many people whose number was ahead of us had been unable to take advantage of it due to the vicissitudes of war. I often wonder what had become of them.

Now we had a chance.

The quota number was not enough. In order to get an American immigration Visa, we had to obtain an affidavit from an American citizen, resident in the United States, who would guarantee that we would not become a public charge and that he would be responsible for us if we failed to support ourselves after reaching the United States. A copy of his most recent tax return had to be attached to the affidavit, to demonstrate that his income was enough to fulfill this guarantee.

My father had business contacts in New York, two brothers from Czechoslovakia, Richard and Zdenek Vogel. They had moved their fur business to the United States many years earlier, and their company, Skins Trading Corporation, was quite successful.

My father wrote to them urgently to ask for an affidavit.

These wonderful people had already issued affidavits to other people to the extent that their incomes permitted, but they found someone for us, a gentleman in Brooklyn, who did not know us of course, but who took the Vogel's word for it that we would not be a burden to him. He filled out the appropriate forms, supplied his tax return. And we had our all-important affidavit.

This was not the only time we were helped by Jews who did not know us, but one of the more important times.

When we got the affidavit, the consul was ready to issue the American visa to us. But now, new problems arose.

The only place in Europe even slightly accessible to us, from which neutral ships left for the United States, was Lisbon, Portugal.

In order to get a Portuguese transit visa, the Portuguese consul in Nice, a nice old gentleman, was required by his government to demand proof that we had transportation onward. Portugal did not want to be overrun by refugees stuck there. A local travel agent issued four tickets for us on the Yankee Clipper, the Pan American plane that made the flight from Lisbon to New York.

Of course, these tickets were fake, and the consul knew it, but the letter of the law was fulfilled. It goes without saying, that we paid the travel agency, and the consul, thus depleting our resources even more.

The next problem was the Spanish transit visa so that we could get to Lisbon. This was the most serious problem, since we had already established that the Spanish did not recognize our Czechoslovak passports.

I discussed this problem with the American vice-consul. He could not have been more helpful. At his suggestion, I typed our vital statistics on four sheets of white bond paper, and he issued an extra copy of the visa on each of these sheets, with a big official-looking ribbon and seal.

We now had to find a Spanish consulate. There was none in Nice; the nearest one was in Marseilles. But in order to be allowed to travel from one city to another in Vichy France, we had to obtain a sauf-conduit –a safe-conduct permit, issued by the Gendarmerie.

I am not sure how it works in other countries, but a Frenchman who has a stamp that you desperately need will make you jump through hoops to get it, just to show his power. And this was not the time and place where we could be anything but meek and compliant.

My father taught me that some money placed into the folds of the Carte d'Identite handed in with the application for the sauf-conduit worked wonders. I have used this technique on other occasions.

French Identity Card

With the sauf-conduit, my father and I travelled to Marseilles, - remember, I was the official interpreter for the family. We presented ourselves at the Spanish consulate with all our documentation, and were told to return in two weeks. Our case could only be decided in two weeks.

Two weeks later, after having gone through the same procedure to get another sauf-conduit to permit us to travel to Marseilles, we appeared at the Spanish consulate. And we received the transit visas on the sheets of bond paper I had typed!

Franco, the Spanish dictator, was a Fascist and an ally of Hitler. Jews who crossed into Spain illegally were interned until the end of the war, but they were not maltreated and Franco did not turn them over to the Germans. By issuing our transit visas on our somewhat questionable documents, he clearly enabled us to save our lives. Do not say anything bad about Franco.

Our final problem to enable us to leave unoccupied France was the biggest one. We needed a French exit visa. In order to obtain this, we had to prove that we did not owe any taxes to the French government. That could only be done by producing a certificate issued by the Banque de France, located at that time, in Chatel-Guyon, a spa near Vichy, where some of the overflow of the French government offices was located.

Foreigners, such as us, were prohibited from traveling to the Vichy area under any circumstances, and no sauf-conduits would be issued.

In a desperation move, my father and I decided to travel without a sauf-conduit, in the full knowledge that there were many inspections, which could result in our arrest and deportation.

We took the train, and hid in the toilets at every stop and whenever we had a hunch that an inspection was imminent.

We arrived in Chatel-Guyon late in the afternoon. We could not go to a hotel, since we had no papers authorizing our presence that we could show. We wandered the streets and saw what used to be a kosher butcher store. My father approached a man emerging from the store, and asked him in Yiddish whether he was Jewish.

The man allowed us to spend the night in his apartment.

This was another incident where a Jew helped out his fellow Jews.

The next morning we got the certificate without any difficulties, and also the exit visas in a ministry office close by. The officials were somewhat astonished at our presence and found no reason not to oblige us. We got back on the train immediately. Following the same procedures, we returned to Nice safely late that night.

Now we could leave.

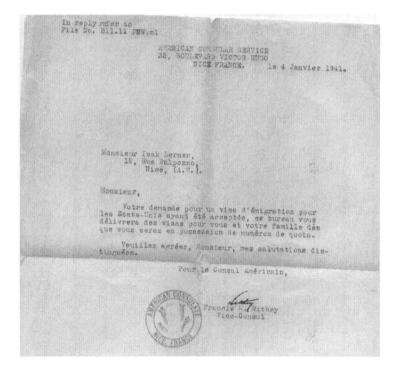

This is a letter issued by the U.S. Vice-Consul in Nice (January 4, 1941) that declared the family would receive a U.S. Immigration Visa. It saved our lives.

CHAPTER 10

On March 15, 1941 we left Nice on a train with its final destination Madrid. It was a long and wearying voyage, with many stops, and many inspections of our papers. But all was well; we crossed into Spain and in due course disembarked in Madrid.

There are two railroad stations in Madrid, one to serve the North and one to serve the South. We had arrived from the North and had to take a taxi to the Atocha Station where we could find the train to Lisbon. The taxi took us across the Gran Via, the main East West corridor through the city. It was a beautiful boulevard, with imposing buildings and many stores. But the view was marred by the numerous flags covering the buildings, not only the Spanish flag, but the German Swastika banner and the Italian flag. Franco demonstrated his gratitude to his Allies for having helped him defeat the Republican side in the Spanish Civil War.

I remember how uncomfortable we felt and how glad we were to board the train to Lisbon. After another day's travel, we arrived in a truly neutral country. Portugal was a dictatorship run by President Salazar, but attempted to maintain strict neutrality.

We found accommodations in a small hotel. And now our major problem had to be dealt with. How do we get to the United States? Both our Portuguese transit visas and our American Immigration visas were set to expire in another month. Rumor – always King Rumor – had it that the Germans would march through their ally Spain to take Gibraltar and thus cut off British access to the Suez Canal and her colonies. If they did that, wouldn't they also take Portugal?

This was a very logical inference and I still do not know why it did not happen. The assumption is that Franco was not as compliant as the Germans wanted, and insisted on remaining neutral.

There was only one ship scheduled to leave for New York in that window of opportunity – The SS Nyassa of the Compania Nacional de Navegacao. Of course, it was impossible to find a berth on that ship.

We needed to find a way to bribe ourselves onto that ship. The fact that none of us spoke Portuguese was an obstacle, but I found that I could use a mixture of French, Latin, German and English to communicate.

We ran all over Lisbon trying to find the "Macher", the man who had access. We went to the steamship offices every day, only to be told by the same young man that there was no space for us.

The Joint Distribution Committee, an American Jewish organization – now part of the United Jewish Appeal – had offices in Lisbon. We were running out of money by then. They promised that they would lend us the money for the ship tickets if we could get them, but they could not help us with anything extra legal, such as bribes, nor did they know whom to bribe. But this meant that practically all the remainder of our funds was available, if we could only find the right contact.

In the meantime, Passover had begun, and we found a kosher restaurant where a communal Seder service was performed. Most of the attendees were refugees like us, from countries that no longer existed because of the German occupation. They were all waiting – for visas, for transport, or for internment by the Portuguese government, because their permits had expired. It was not a cheerful Seder, but perhaps more meaningful because of the circumstances.

The time for the departure of the Nyassa was approaching and we still had no hope. We knew that if we did not get on this ship, we would be interned by the Portuguese when our visas expired, and what would happen to us if, indeed, the Germans invaded, did not bear thinking about.

One day we were sitting in a café on the Placa Rossio, a café that was frequented by Jewish refugees, and my twelve-year-old sister Susi overheard people at the table next to us talk about the contact they had found.

This is how we found the "Macher". The day before the Nyassa was scheduled to sail, he got us two tickets. We decided to send Susi and my mother into safety. The morning of the departure, we got two more tickets for my father and me. It took almost all the rest of the cash we had, and true to their promise, the Joint advanced the money for the tickets.

This was money given anonymously by Jews to help other Jews, and we were the beneficiaries. Is it any wonder that I feel a sense of obligation to our people?

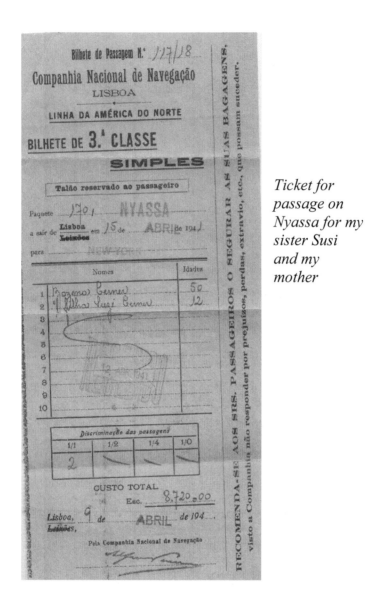

Ticket for passage on Nyassa for my sister Susi and my mother

When we walked up the gangplank, there was the young man who had turned us down every day, collecting tickets. Our eyes met, but no words were exchanged. In my heart, I had a sense of triumph, relief and apprehension.

My mother, who had been a rock throughout our three years on the road, suddenly collapsed. In the last minute, she did not want to go. After all, she said, who went to America? – Only gangsters and failures who could not make it in Europe. She was a European. I think she realized then what we had known for a long time, that she would never again be the lady she had been in Vienna, living in an apartment decorated by Feuer, with household help, and wealth and comfort.

Of course it did not take long, and she was her old self again, brave and cheerful and only concerned about the safety and comfort of her family.

On April 5, 1941 the SS Nyassa left Lisbon, crowded to overflowing with refugees. We were in steerage, of course, three bunks on top of each other and hundreds of people crowded into each hold. When I went back to Europe as an American soldier less than three years later, our hammocks aboard the troop transport were five high; in comparison to that, the Nyassa was relatively luxurious.

Leaving Lisbon on the river Tagus and entering the Atlantic Ocean, the small ship encountered heavy seas, and a lot of people got seasick.

My mother and sister were in the part of the steerage reserved for women. My father and I were in the hold for males. I could not stay there and listen and watch – and smell – the results of seasickness. I told my father that I would see him in the morning, and spent the night in an armchair in the second-class lounge.

The next morning, the first and second-class sections were made off limits for the steerage passengers. But on the open sea, seasickness abated for most people. There were so many extra passengers on the ship that there was not enough food. We got one meal a day, and an apple a day. We did not care. We were on our way to safety.

Nyassa, Portugal

Because of the fear of submarines, the ship was lit up day and night, and festooned with big Portuguese flags, and the words Portugal – Neutral, whenever possible.

After a ten-day voyage, on Friday, April 25, 1941, we were scheduled to dock in New York.

I did not want to miss the sight of the Statue of Liberty, and stayed on deck the whole night before our arrival. At dawn I had my first sight not only of the Statue but also of the skyscrapers of downtown New York. We landed in Brooklyn. Immigration officers came aboard to check our papers. This procedure took most of the day, but I noticed that they were polite and treated us as human beings, quite differently from the way we had been treated in Europe.

Some reporters came aboard and interviewed and photographed some passengers. Apparently, this was one of the last ships to bring refugees from war-torn Europe.

Several months later, I found a photo in the now defunct newspaper PM, and I am easily recognizable by those who know me well, wearing a hat and looking happy.

And then we stepped on the soil of our new country.

From that moment on, I was a patriotic and devoted American, grateful for the safety that this wonderful country afforded us.

My father's business friend, Richard Vogel, came to pick us up. He lent my father some cash, and took us by taxi to the Hotel Excelsior on West 79th Street near Columbus Avenue. We had not eaten all day, and found that there was a Jewish delicatessen around the corner. We had the best meal of our lives, not only because we were hungry, but also because it was the kind of Jewish food we had not eaten in a very long time.

And then we slept for the first time in more than three years without worrying about a knock at the door.

The next morning, Saturday, my father said that it was time that we went to a synagogue. We had so much to be thankful for. We were alive and safe. The hotel staff directed us to a large building close by. We walked in, and, to our horror, saw that the congregation wore no skullcaps, that there was organ music, and that men and women sat together. We thought it was a church. This was our introduction to Reform Judaism.

A congregant who saw our shock, directed us to an orthodox synagogue nearby, and we were able to pray, as we had been accustomed to. My father approached the Rabbi, and a special prayer of thanks was pronounced on our behalf.

We were safe in our new home.

CHAPTER 11

And now we began our new life in America.

The first thing we did was take a trip to Brooklyn to thank the gentleman who had given us our affidavit. We also reassured him that he would never have to be responsible for us.

We found an apartment on the Westside of Manhattan, on 100th Street between Columbus and Amsterdam Avenues, flanked by a police station and a garage, The apartment was in a brownstone, a three flight walk-up. It was small and not decorated by Feuer, but it was home and we were safe.

The area has since been razed and transformed into a huge development, but our brownstone was not so different from many streets of brownstones on the West Side.

We had no money. We had debts. First of all, we owed money to Richard Vogel, who had picked us up at the pier and lent us enough to get us started. Then, we owed money to the Joint Distribution Committee who had advanced us the funds for our tickets on the

Nyassa. But we were not poor; we just did not have any money.

My father was 51 years old, I was 16 ½. We had no doubt about our ability to survive. While we had no money, we still felt that we were in the middle class, regardless of how we lived and what we did for a living.

In those days, there was a surplus of apartments in New York. Moving day was November 1, I believe. Thus, if you signed a lease earlier you often got free rent, called concession, until November 1. That was certainly helpful.

We bought basic furniture, to be paid over twenty-four months.

I then had the most miraculous experience – I found the New York Public Library. There was a branch right near us. They gave me a library card without question, and I could borrow books! The first book I borrowed was "Alice in Wonderland". That was a mistake; the book is filled with puns and word play, and my English was inadequate for an appreciation of Lewis Carroll's work. Still, I enjoyed it. And I did not have to steal books any more. From then on, the library became my second home.

My English was good enough to read books, but very limited as far as ordinary conversation was concerned. The vast difference on how you pronounce a word and how you spell it, caused me a lot of trouble, and it took a while before I could speak my new language.

Since I was under 18, I had to get working papers and did so, and we all got social security cards. Here again, my encounter with the bureaucrats who issued these documents was positive.

And one of our first visits was to the Department of Immigration and Naturalization, then located on Columbus Circle, where we filed our Declaration of Intent to become American citizens – our "first papers". In five years we would be entitled to apply for citizenship.

Then we went to the H.I.A.S. – the Hebrew Immigrant Aid Society, located on Lafayette Street, in the building that now houses the Public Theater. There, they lent my father $ 3000.00 without collateral or interest, so that he could get back into business.

This was another instance where we were helped by the donations of anonymous Jews. I do not want to harp on this issue, but I need to make the point that my experiences have imposed an obligation on me to repay. The HIAS and the United Jewish Appeal have been first in my schedule of contributions from the moment I could afford to make them.

I understand that HIAS made many such loans and that all of them were repaid. I know that we did not go to a movie – with one exception – or spent money on entertainment, until my father could pay back what we owed, first to the Vogels and then to HIAS and to the Joint.

The exception was Charlie Chaplin's film "The Great Dictator". The fact that one could make fun of Hitler and Mussolini and get away with it without being murdered seemed another miracle to us.

The $3000.00 my father borrowed was a great deal of money in those days. The subway was 5 cents – today it is $2.50. My first salary was $ 8.00 per week.

I got a job in a fur store on West 86th Street sweeping up, making deliveries, beating fur coats to get the dust out of them and making myself generally useful.

Another wonderful thing happened to me while we were waiting in the offices of HIAS. A beautiful girl my age came up to me, and said :"Aren't you…". Her name was Gerda Kominik, and she had lived around the corner from me in Vienna. When I was thirteen, in Vienna, I had had no interest in girls and did not remember her at all. Now, however, I had reached the tender age of puberty, and instantly fell in love with all examples of young womanhood that I encountered. During our travels in Europe, I had had no contact with young women, and I felt a great desire to remedy this flaw.

Gerda informed me that a group of Viennese refugee kids our age usually met in a Ping-Pong Hall on 96th Street and Broadway every Friday.

That Friday, I slicked back my hair and went there intending to impress everyone with my suave and debonair manner as a world traveller.

Indeed, I met a number of young people there, all refugees from Vienna, and some of whom are still friends today. We all had stories of survival, so that topic did not have to be discussed. We all had similar backgrounds, and more in common than with American kids of our age, and so we formed a support group that lasted for a long time.

That evening an incident occurred that my wife Lenore loved to tell to her "English as a second language" students.

In my suave and debonair manner, I mentioned that something was quite ob-VI-ous. Ob-VI-ously, ob-VI-ous should be pronounced ob-VI-ous. General laughter embarrassed me considerably, and I found that I was not quite as suave and debonair as I had hoped.

My father, with the help of my mother, opened a store at 200 West 28th Street, in the heart of the Fur District. In those days, the fur business was totally Jewish, and Yiddish was the language of the business. My parents started to learn English, but did not need it to conduct business.

In Vienna, my father had dealt in "noble" furs. Now, he could not afford to do so. He dealt in Persian lamb paws and remnants. Persian lamb coats were very popular then. My father went to the furriers making those coats, and bought the remnants – the pieces left over after a fur had been cut. He then sorted them according to quality and sold them to other furriers who made coats out of them for a much cheaper trade. My father considered this business a major comedown from what he had been doing in Vienna, but he did well in it. He was a very good businessman.

Today the fur business is mainly Greek-owned. Apparently, the children of the Jews who controlled the fur business then, did not want to stay in it. They became doctors and lawyers and went into other fields, and so the Greeks took it over. A microcosm of America.

For immediate additional cash, my parents found a manufacturer of hairnets, who needed to have the hairnets inserted into individual envelopes for sale in lower end department stores. Today, I suppose this would be done mechanically.

We picked up cartons of hairnets and cartons of envelopes, and we all-including my twelve-year-old sister Susi, sat around the kitchen table every spare minute we had, and inserted hairnets into the envelopes. I do not know how much we got for every thousand envelopes, but we kept doing this until all our debts had been repaid. That took about eighteen months.

After a few weeks, I was sufficiently Americanized and my conversational English had improved enough, that I could get another job: I started to work for a manufacturer of costume jewelry as a shipping clerk. My duties included packaging, shipping, making deliveries and of course sweeping up and doing whatever else I was told to do. The costume jewelry district was around 23rd street then. My salary was $ 12.00 per week.

My boss had a patent – a plastic comb called "Quirl" comb, which was supposed to take Woolworth and other five-and-dime stores by storm. He gave up the costume jewelry business and concentrated on packing and shipping these combs. As my experience in packing and shipping increased, so did my salary.

Unfortunately, after a burst of activity, Woolworth stopped buying. My boss went out of business, and I learned a valuable lesson about business in general.

I found another job as shipping clerk with a manufacturer of general merchandise, also destined to Five and Dime stores, and I kept that job until I entered the U.S. Army in May of 1943. By that time I'm proud to say, I made $25.00 per week.

In September of 1941 the school year began, and it was time to continue our education. Susi started regular school, but I had to find a school with evening classes so that I could continue working. The New York Evening High School was designed for exactly my circumstances. It was located on west 65th Street, where the Lincoln Center complex now stands.

Classes were held from 7 p.m. until 10 p.m. I would go directly from work, have a sandwich somewhere, and after school a whole bunch of us students would walk home together. Many of the students were refugees in exactly the same position that I was, and quite a few lived on the West Side. The walk home was generally very pleasant and it saved the 5 cents subway fare. Most lived closer than I, and I usually had the last 10-12 blocks to myself.

At that time, there were three kinds of High School diplomas: the Academic Diploma entitling you to admission to college, a Vocational Diploma, showing the hours you had spent in shop in various disciplines and a General Diploma. Regardless of our financial condition, I do not believe that it occurred to me or to my parents for one second that Susi and I would not go to college.

The New York Evening High School administrators were very understanding and cooperative. I was allowed to take a number of Regents Examinations without ever having taken any classes in the United States. I had no trouble passing Regents in French, German, European History and Geography, with honors, and I took a chance on Math and passed it as well, even though Math in France was taught quite differently.

The courses I took were English, American History and a course called Civics, which, I suppose, today is called Social Studies. Upon passing the Regents in these coursers as well, I had my Academic Diploma in June of 1942.

Now to backtrack a little:

The war had continued even after our departure from Europe. The Germans conquered the Balkans, including Greece (in the process killing my Aunt Ella and her husband). The Afrika Corps under the command of General – later Field Marshall -- Rommel threatened the Suez Canal.

In June of 1941, Germany invaded the Soviet Union.

Before long, German troops had overrun the Ukraine and the remnant of Poland occupied by the Soviets in 1939. German troops stood at the gates of Leningrad, Moscow and Stalingrad, and controlled the vital Southern sector of the Soviet Union, where its oil and food were produced.

Almost all the Jews on the continent of Europe were now under German control, and there was nowhere for them to go.

In the United States, we knew that it was only a matter of time before the war reached us, and I could hardly wait to join the Army and return to Europe as an American soldier. I am sure that my parents did not share these feelings; now that I am a parent and grandparent I can appreciate that.

On December 7, 1941, the Japanese, allies of Germany, attacked the American Naval Base of

Pearl Harbor in Hawaii and destroyed a major portion of the U.S. Pacific Fleet. Germany and Italy declared war on the United States. Now it was truly a World War.

The group of Viennese refugee kids, who had met at the Ping-Pong place, had increased to a couple of hundred, enough to create a formal club, called the Austrian Youth. A loft was found on West100[th] Street, right across from our apartment, and because of the size of the membership, the club was organized into two groups, the Wednesday Group for people in their twenties, and the Friday group for the late teens, to which I belonged.

We would get together on Friday evenings for games, discussions and amateur theatricals, and on Sunday go to Van Cortland Park for soccer, and in the summer go to Jacob Riis Park to the beach.

After a while, I began to be bothered by the fact that there was too much talk about our going back to Austria after the war, to create a socialist Austrian state. Particularly Curt Ponger, who was somewhat older and the leader of the Wednesday group, and Otto Verber, a leader of the Friday group, constantly brought the discussions around to this point. I started to agitate that we were Americans and Jewish, and that we should not be interested in

Austria which had kicked us out, but that our future lay in America as American Jews.

There was a big general meeting of the Friday group, and under the leadership of Ponger and Verber, I was expelled. The two sergeants-at-arms, who escorted me out, were George Stein and Freddy Reiss, both among my oldest and dearest friends.

By that time, I had enough friends outside the club. In any case, within a few months, most of the boys in the club were in the service.

After the war, when we all came back – at least those of us, who made it safely - there were some casualties- my dear friends had seen the light. When the club was revived in early 1946, there was a revolution, and most of my friends, led by George Stein, broke away to form a new club – the Freedom Club, to which I was immediately invited and which functioned on the principles I had mentioned, that we were Americans and Jews. George has been my friend and my accountant for most of my life. He was President of his Synagogue, and has been the most loyal of Americans. But I will not let him live down his earlier immaturity.

In 1945 I was in Paris on a three-day pass, and I ran into Otto Verber on the steps of the Madeleine. When I greeted him happily, he wanted to know the date of my commission to determine who was senior and had to salute the other. I am afraid I responded in a manner my parents would have disapproved.

The interesting thing is that this attitude of submission to authority makes you very vulnerable to a statist philosophy. A few years later, Otto Verber and Curt Ponger were arrested as spies for the Soviet Union, were tried and convicted, served several years in prison and were then expelled to Austria.

A few years ago, George Stein organized a fifty-year reunion of the club. Many people showed up. What I found very appealing is the fact that most of us had arrived in the United States without a penny, but all had been very successful in creating good, decent and prosperous lives in this great country.

The club was very important to me. The people there had similar backgrounds as Jewish refugees from Vienna; we each had our own stories and therefore we understood each other. We did not feel foreign or exotic among ourselves, and shared language and cultural backgrounds. Among the friends I met and retained throughout the years were not only George Stein and his wife Carol, but also Paul and Anita Goldberger, Paul and Susi Schwarzkopf, Peter and Susi Orne, John and Alice Morawetz, and above all, Julianna Glass, who became my first wife and the mother of my children. Sadly, many of them are gone by now.

And now, back to my story.

In the fall of 1942, armed with my academic diploma, I entered college – City College at 137th Street and Convent Avenue. Here too, it was possible to take courses at night, and my routine of going to school from work continued. CCNY did not require a tuition payment from New York City residents, but I had to pay for books and incidental expenses. This time, however, I took the subway back. There were no more walks home.

By that time, my father's business had prospered. The debts had been repaid, and we moved to a much nicer apartment at 309 West 99th Street, between West End Avenue and Riverside Drive. This was an elevator building and we lived on a high floor.

We had a large living room, in which there was a pullout couch for my sister Susi, a den with a pullout couch for me, and a nice bedroom for my parents with an airy eat-in kitchen. We acquired more furniture, and while it was not anywhere near the apartment my mother had lost in Vienna, it was perfectly adequate and it was our home.

CHAPTER 12

On my eighteenth birthday, September 4, 1942, I filled out a form waiving my rights not to be drafted as a Czech citizen (considered an ally of the United States), and requested immediate induction into the Armed Forces of the United States.

Had I not done so, I could not have lived with myself. This was my war and I wanted to get my own back.

It is odd, what moments remain with you. I remember very clearly standing in a news shop at 104th Street and Broadway, waiting for the owner, who was a notary public, to notarize my signature on those documents. Judy Garland was singing "Embraceable you" on the radio, and I remember thinking that this was a moment that would change my life very drastically once again.

In spite of my request for immediate induction, the Army took its time. It was not until March of 1943 that I was called for a physical examination. I believe that if you could walk into the military doctor's office under your own steam, you were classified I-A. Shortly thereafter I was called for induction. City College suggested that I apply for a two months deferment so that I could complete the term, and the Army cooperated.

In May 1943, five years after leaving Vienna, I reported for duty at Pennsylvania Station. There, a whole bunch of us were sworn in, and I was a soldier in the Army of the United States.

My parents and sister accompanied me to the railroad station, and we said a tearful farewell. We had managed to be together for the three years of our Odyssey until we reached our new home, but now I went off to new adventures all alone.

The first stop as a soldier was Fort Dix, New Jersey. There I was issued military uniforms and equipment, and shipped my civilian clothes back to New York.

I was excited by the new adventures awaiting me and exhilarated by the thought of being able to pay the Germans back for what they had done. I know, now that I am a parent and grandparent, that my parents' feelings were quite different. They, much more than I, were aware of the risks of war and were worried about me.

The first and most important lesson I learned as a soldier was to salute everything that moves and to obey everyone who yelled, since I was at the lowest end of the totem pole.

I learned another valuable lesson about volunteering in the Army. I was determined to be a good soldier, and so when they called for volunteers, I spoke up. I was given a baton, and was required to walk my post for four hours in the middle of the camp, while my companions from the train lounged around, drinking cokes and coffee.

Later on, during my service, I volunteered on several occasions, but only when I was convinced of their purpose.

In Fort Dix, the Army also tested my abilities in a somewhat cursory manner. I was told that there would be further tests during basic training. In any case, after three or four days in Fort Dix, I was put on a troop train to Camp Picket, Virginia. This was a huge army camp near the small town of Blackstone, Virginia, which was overwhelmed by the sudden presence of thousands of soldiers.

In Camp Picket I found myself assigned to a Medical Replacement Training Depot for basic training. Well, my parents wanted me to be a doctor, but I don't think they had planned on my being an army medic.

Basic training was supposed to last twelve weeks and make a soldier out of a civilian. I started out learning close order drill, calisthenics, obstacle courses and all the military necessities such as ranks and how to salute them, general orders for guard duty, and kitchen police – the famous K.P.

In addition, - this was in the days before penicillin- there were detailed instructions on how to administer prophylactics, and there were a number of Army training films, notably what we called Mickey Mouse films, that would scare you away from ever having sex. In those days, acquiring a venereal disease (today they are called sexually transmitted diseases) was a court-martial offense, and the Army made a major effort to protect us against ourselves.

I was taught that there would be "Prophylactic Stations" near all Army Camps. All soldiers who went on leave had to carry a condom with them, and if they had sex they were required to report to a prophylactic station and have a medic administer a series of steps involving syringes, creams and soap and water in a very precise order.

When I was in London, a year later, such a Prophylactic Station was on the upper floor of a building on Piccadilly Circus. It did not endear us with our British Allies.

I reflected that I had not enlisted to spend my time supervising soldiers' attempts to eradicate the results of very natural behavior.

During this time, I was called in for more tests. First I had an IQ test, which showed a very satisfactory number. Then my knowledge of French and German and recent European history were evaluated.

Three weeks after beginning basic training, I was pulled out of that unit and transferred to the Military Intelligence Training Center at Camp Ritchie, Maryland.

Perhaps it is because the Army did not take enough time to make a soldier out of me, that I always remained a civilian at heart.

Camp Ritchie was a small camp in the mountains of Western Maryland, beautifully located, surrounding a small lake. A Colonel Banfill, an old time army man who, I believe, had some problems coping with a wave of intellectual Europeans, was in command.

First, according to an ironclad rule, new arrivals had one week of K.P. In addition, Colonel Banfill had learned a lesson from the Sunday attack on Pearl Harbor. He therefore instituted a system whereby we worked for eight days and then had a day off; in other words, the day off was Monday one week, Tuesday the next week, then Wednesday and so forth. Naturally, the day off became known as Ban-Day.

In Camp Pickett, I had bunked with people from all over America, including some hillbillies whom I had lots of trouble understanding. On the other hand, Camp Ritchie was filled with the caliber of people I was very comfortable with.

Professor Lehmann, my professor of religion at the Akademische Gymnasium in Vienna, peeled potatoes next to me. Even though we were both privates in the U.S.Army, to me he was still the Herr Professor and I could not treat him as an army buddy. There was a famous author, Stefan Heym, who after the war returned to Germany. Just recently I came across his autobiography in which he described his stay in Camp Ritchie. His description was right on target.

There was a cadre of instructors, and there were classes in all kinds of esoteric subjects. Of course, this was still a military operation, and we had close order drill, calisthenics and an obstacle course that had to be conquered, invariably, the first thing in the morning after Ban-Day. In addition, we practiced, blindfolded, the care and disassembly and reassembly of the M-1 rifle.

The principal courses of study were order of battle: familiarity with every rank, unit, insignia, weapons and organization in the German and Italian armies; codes and ciphers, explosives, Morse code (my worst subject), radio communication, map reading, and background studies on conditions in occupied Europe.

Every once in a while, we would be dropped off in the middle of the night in some unfamiliar corner of Maryland, with a map and an azimuth and instructions to get to a certain destination within a fixed time period. At times, we were captured by soldiers from the permanent cadre wearing German uniforms. They put us through long periods of interrogation without damaging us too much. At times, we did the interrogating. We played games wearing different uniforms and practiced hiding out behind enemy lines.

The Army had a system of classifications, which appeared in your service record, and then, in theory, enabled the personnel department to place you where you could do the most good. After taking all the appropriate courses Camp Ritchie had to offer, I was classified as Interrogator of Prisoners of War (IPM), Military Intelligence Interpreter (MII), Order of Battle Analyst (OB) and Military Intelligence Operative (MIO).

I had a wonderful time.

Once in a while, on Ban-Day, I went to New York. This meant a taxi shared by several of us, two hours drive to Baltimore and a train from there to New york. I would arrive by 10 or 11 PM. Then, I could let my mother spoil me for a day, and I returned the next evening to be back in camp in time for the obstacle course.

I had a girl friend - Eva Morgan - when I left for the Army, and for the first few Ban-Days she would meet me to spend the rest of the evening with me. But she had a full time job, and could not stay up late during the week merely because I wanted to be entertained. So, by mutual agreement, we called it off. Of course I blamed Colonel Banfill for the end of that romance.

My salary as a private was $ 21.00 per month. There was a popular song " $21.00 per day once a month". I had few expenses. The Army provided clothing, food and shelter, and the general population was extremely nice to men in uniform. Once in a while, the U.S.O. organized a dance, and young women from the neighboring towns were brought in. I suspect that in spite of all the warnings, romance flourished here and there.

The United States Government decided that it would not be fair to send someone overseas to fight for this country without making him a citizen. So, on September 18, 1943, at the Circuit Court of Washington County in Hagerstown, Maryland, I took the oath and became an American citizen. It was only two and a half years after I had arrived in the United States. The oath was very meaningful to me. I was very proud to be a citizen. I finally had a country again.

When my parents and my sister became citizens in 1946, after the war, I as an American citizen was able to be a witness for them.

A small patriotic digression:

This is the best country in the world. It was difficult to get here, and I arrived without a penny and in fact, in debt. But this country gave me every opportunity to obtain an education, to make a very comfortable living, and to bring up three wonderful children. Bismarck said, nations have no friends, they have only interests. This is brutally true for most countries, but less so for the United States. I firmly believe that this is the only country that wants to do the right not only the expedient thing, and that there is a strong streak of altruism that affects our actions.

I am very proud to be an American.

The summer and fall of 1943 passed pleasantly in Camp Ritchie. We were told that upon completion of all the courses, we would be commissioned and assigned to various units as intelligence officers.

But that did not happen.

Colonel Banfill, who apparently, desperately, wanted to be a general, kept bringing in more and more soldiers for training, even some whose language skills were totally inadequate. At the same time, there did not seem to be a demand for the highly trained graduates of the Camp Ritchie courses, even though preparations were being made for an invasion of the continent of Europe. There was a bottleneck. Camp Ritchie was getting overcrowded.

The solution was Camp Sharpe, Pennsylvania. During the great depression the government created summer camps for the Civilian Conversation Corps.

Young people were hired to work on roads and in forests to keep them off the street. Sharpe was such a camp. It was about thirty miles from Camp Ritchie.

A number of graduates, like myself, who had completed all the classes Camp Ritchie had to offer, were transferred to Camp Sharpe. We hiked there with full field packs, and found a place strictly designed for summer occupation. Unfortunately, by that time it was winter, and a very snowy and cold winter at that. I do not believe that I was ever as cold, as walking a tour of guard duty in the snow there, not even during the Battle of the Bulge a year later.

At Camp Sharpe we resumed infantry training in full force. The Gettysburg National Battlefield was not far, and even though the battle of Gettysburg was fought during three hot July days, I remember the battlefield from hiking all over it in snow and ice.

Camp Sharpe was one of my least pleasant experiences. I spent about two months there.

Finally, in February of 1944, word came through that we would be shipped overseas. A large group, most of the Camp Sharpe residents plus some more recent graduates, was sent to the Port of Embarkation at Fort Hamilton, Brooklyn.

And there we sat, waiting to ship out.

Every evening, I got a pass to go home to visit my parents. Then I would go out into the city to enjoy myself. Once, my sister and I were going to a movie in the theater district, and someone came up to us and gave us orchestra tickets for a Broadway Show. People were very nice to soldiers.

I would go to sleep in my own bed, get up at 5 AM so that I could report back to Fort Hamilton by 7 AM, lounge around Fort Hamilton the whole day, and return home that night for dinner.

Of course, I never knew when we would board our ship and leave for Europe and the war, so every time I left in the morning, it was a tearful farewell, and then I was home again that night. I am sure that there came a point when my parents must have felt: Go, already!

One day, a group of Jewish soldiers, which included me, went to the Rabbi in Fort Hamilton, and said some prayers to safeguard us on our voyage. And, maybe it helped. After all, I returned home safely.

In any case, after four weeks at the Port of Embarkation, I did not come home for dinner. We were put on alert, prevented from making any phone calls home, and boarded a Victory ship.

These were small cargo ships built in a hurry by our shipyards just for the war. We were in a convoy of about twenty vessels, surrounded and guarded by destroyers.

If I had thought that the Nyassa was crowded, I did not know what crowded meant. We slept in our clothes in hammocks five high. We shared our hammocks with our duffle bags, our helmets and our rifles. We were required to wear life vests at all times. Most of our time was spent standing in line for meals and bathroom facilities.

It was mid March and the Atlantic was fairly rough. There was quite a bit of seasickness around, which made the atmosphere less than pleasant.

We had no idea where we would land, but after about ten days of travel we landed in Belfast, in Northern Ireland. Trucks took us to the estate of Lord Londonderry, near Derry, where a huge camp was set up, a replacement depot, or "repple depple" in army parlance.

Here is a photo on the ship: I am the tall
soldier.

CHAPTER 13

The function of a replacement depot was just that. When the invasion finally took place and there were casualties, replacements would be brought in from the "repple depples" according to their Army Classifications. In the meantime, our job was to wait.

The group from Camp Ritchie, by now known as the "cattle alert", found out to our horror, that in order to get rid of this surplus of men, Colonel Banfill had added to our classification the classification for I & R Platoon. This was easy for him, because I and R means Intelligence and Reconnaissance. However it had nothing to do with the training we had received. I & R platoon members were the most highly trained combat infantry troops who would go ahead of an advancing army in order to spy out the terrain and, if possible, the enemy positions.

They were of course also the most vulnerable units. I had no objection to putting myself in harm's way. I was idealistic and young and desperately anxious to get back at the Germans. However, I wanted to be in a position to use the skills I had and the training I had received.

At the replacement depot there was no training but merely waiting around. At one point, I organized some classes in French, and a number of people, including some of the higher-ranking officers joined to get the basics.

Of course the first thing they all wanted to know, was the way you could ask a French girl for sex. After I taught them:"Voulez vous coucher avec moi?" we could proceed with more mundane phrases.

We were housed in large tents. In the far distance was the castle of Lord Londonderry, which was off limits to us.

One day, I received permission to leave the camp. A buddy and I walked around the town of Derry. There was a small hotel, and we went in and were served lunch at a table with white tablecloth and gleaming silver utensils. I felt like a human being for the first time in weeks.

And then, an opportunity arose for me to take action.

A man dressed in Officer's Uniform, but without insignia of rank, came to the replacement depot looking for French speaking volunteers. He announced that he represented the O.S.S. – the Office of Strategic Services.

Eventually this is what I found out:

The United States had no strategic intelligence service between World War I and II. The last code-breaking unit the Army had was dissolved when Cordell Hull was Secretary of the Army. Hull famously said at the time: "Gentlemen do not read each other's mail." Hull was the quintessential WASP and those were, perhaps, more innocent days.

As war approached, President Roosevelt appointed General "Wild " Bill Donovan to form an active intelligence unit, the Office of Strategic Services, or OSS, which became the predecessor of the CIA.

The kind of intelligence that we had trained for in Camp Ritchie was essentially battlefield intelligence. By interrogating prisoners of war, by interviewing civilians close to the battlefield, and perhaps by sneaking across the lines for more information, we could hopefully obtain intelligence about the enemy's dispositions that would be helpful to our commanders.

Strategic intelligence takes a much longer view. Its practitioners attempt to find out first, the enemies abilities, and then his intentions. His intentions may be to invade a certain island, but if he does not have enough ships, that won't work. Similarly, a sudden influx of naval vessels in one area may predict an action of that sort. While this is a gross simplification, I hope it explains the difference between strategic and tactical intelligence.

In addition, strategic intelligence includes, in wartime, sabotage and other underground activities.

With little background in strategic intelligence, the OSS used British Intelligence as mentor and guide. The British, of course, had centuries of experience.

By the time the OSS representative showed up, I had been in the replacement depot in Northern Ireland for several weeks.

After I appeared as a potential volunteer, the OSS representative explained that they were looking for people trained in intelligence to parachute into occupied France to work with the French underground in preparation for the invasion.

I volunteered.

Why did I do that? Of course, I was nineteen years old and like all nineteen year old youngsters, I was immortal. And I was anxious to fight against Germany. But with the hindsight of maturity, I attribute this decision to abysmal stupidity.

Two other Ritchie graduates volunteered, both of them native Frenchmen, with families in France, which they hoped to see.

Orders were cut. This phrase shows you how antediluvian World War II must appear to the generation of computers and cell phones. It refers to mimeograph sheets. There were special typewriters and special mimeograph paper. The typewriters would cut the letters into the paper. Then the paper would be mounted on a mimeograph machine, consisting essentially of a roller and ink. As many copies as necessary were created by turning the roller.

We each received one copy of the order transferring us to a mysteriously numbered Army unit, and instructing us to report within four days to an address on Shaftesbury Avenue in Central London.

We caught a ride to the port of Belfast. There we reported to the port commandant, who, upon seeing our orders, put us on a ferry across the Irish Sea to Britain. There, we caught a train to London and reported to the address we had been given.

First we were informed that we had been transferred to the O.S.S. Then we were told that upon pain of death and eternal torture, we were not to reveal any information about the

OSS and our actions within that organization. We took an oath to that effect.

I am now faced with a dilemma. The war is long over and it is highly likely that most if not all the people I dealt with, friends and enemies are no longer with us. Yet, I took an oath, and I will attempt to keep my promise.

In London, we left our American uniforms in that apartment- there were many duffle bags and suitcases stored there. I wondered whether they belonged to people who had already gone into occupied France.

We dressed in the uniforms of British subalterns with one pip on each shoulder. From then on, we were in the hands of our British allies.

We were taken to an estate somewhere outside of London – one of the stately homes of England. First, I was required to write an autobiography in French, German and English. Then, some of the skills we had learned at Camp Ritchie were tested – Morse code was my worst subject. For the next two weeks we were given what I can only call espionage training, codes, ciphers, signals, unarmed combat, and subjects too esoteric to describe.

And then, one lovely spring morning, I was taken to an airfield, to be taught how to parachute from a plane.

I had never been on a plane in my life. I was given a parachute with the usual joke: "Don't worry, if it doesn't work, just bring it back and we'll exchange it." I was told to count to ten before pulling the ripcord, so that my chute would not be tangled in the propeller. I was also told to bend my knees when I hit the ground and to roll. And finally, I was told that landing is like jumping from the second floor of a building.

We then boarded the plane and it took off. We drew lots, and I was scheduled to jump last. My two companions managed to do it, and then it was my turn. I stood in the open door of the plane, the wind beating my face, and I held on for dear life to the doorjamb, completely frozen.

The jump sergeant, accustomed to the fear shown by first-timers, gave me a tremendous kick where it did the most good. I can still feel the imprint of his boot on my lower back. I literally flew out of the plane, grabbed the ripcord and pulled. I certainly did not count to ten. I found myself praying that the chute would open and it did. All I had to do was to hold on. I was suddenly jerked upright when the chute opened and filled with air. The ground approached far faster than I had anticipated. I curled up in a ball, as instructed, and hit the ground hard, rolled a bit and there I was, bruised, but alive.

This was one of my least favored experiences. I do not ever want to do it again.

When I stumbled away from the landing field, another soldier scheduled to jump, approached me and asked: " How was it?'

"Piece of cake," I lied.

After a few more days of training, two Free French Officers came around to interview us. When they spoke with me, they said, that while my French was certainly excellent, I spoke with an accent. I could never pass for a native born Frenchman. There were too many French collaborators; any one could put me in danger.

I returned to London on my own and reported back to the apartment on Shaftesbury Avenue. There I changed back into my American uniform. A middle-aged civilian sat down with me to discuss my future.

Of course I know his name, but as indicated above, I will keep my confidentially commitment as much as possible.

He told me that I had placed them in a quandary. " We cannot send you into occupied France, and there is no time to work on your accent. But you could be a very valuable asset to us once the balloon goes up – (the then current phrase for the beginning of the invasion of Europe). Go back to your outfit. We will know where you are and we will call on you when we need you. You will keep your membership in the OSS secret – of course."

My two French companions stayed behind, and I have no idea what ever happened to them. I was again given appropriate travel orders. I persuaded the clerk who issued them to give me a week's travel time to get back to the estate of Lord Londonderry.

This meant that I had a day or two in London.

On Grosvenor Square, next to where the U.S. Embassy now stands, there is a building, which, then, was the headquarters of ETOUSA – European Theater of Operations, United States Army. It was the headquarters of General Eisenhower, who had been named supreme commander of Operation Overlord, the anticipated invasion of the continent.

I was a 19 ½ year old private, but I had Chutzpah. I went to this imposing building and asked to speak to the G-2, the chief of staff for Military Intelligence. A full Colonel came out to talk to me. I explained to him that I had been trained in a number of military intelligence disciplines at Camp Ritchie, that I spoke French and German, and that I was presently in a replacement depot and did not want to wait, but wanted to get into the war now, and I asked him for a job.

Amazingly enough, he listened, wrote down my Army Serial Number, and the exact military address of my unit in Northern Ireland, and promised to do something for me.

I was not sure that this would happen, but I felt that I had done all I could.

I also had a chance to visit my Aunt Regina and my cousin Monica, who lived in Golders Green, a lovely suburb of London. They were enormously pleased to see me, particularly in an American uniform. Then I made my way back to Northern Ireland by train, ferry and bus.

When I arrived at the replacement depot, I was told that the Camp Ritchie "cattle alert" had been transferred to a Camp near Chester, England.

Immediately, I returned to England. The Ferry across the Irish Sea in the late spring is anything but pleasant, and this was my third trip.   Fortunately, I am not subject to seasickness.

I took a train to Chester, hitchhiked to the Camp, and reported for duty.

Here again, nothing happened for a while. I resumed my activities teaching French to all comers, and spent some time, whenever I could get permission, to wander around Chester. This is a charming, medieval cathedral town along a lovely river. I enjoyed the town very much.

I found that the British, particularly, the British young women I met, were very hospitable and welcoming.

And then, my colonel came through for me. Orders came in, transferring me to G-2 of ETOUSA in London.

I reported for duty in the building where I had met my colonel, and was assigned quarters nearby. I was in London on the eve of the invasion of the continent.

The first of these photos shows me on Piccadilly Circus. The familiar statue of Eros is covered with protective material against potential damage from bombs. The other picture is me visiting my aunt and cousin.

I cannot describe the atmosphere of the city – it was electric, and if you wore a uniform, you owned the town. I was able to spend some more time with my aunt Regina and my cousin Monica, and I also met my cousin Kurt Deutscher. He had been invalided out of the British Army in Palestine, and was now a waiter at the Strand Palace Hotel. He was married and had a small daughter.

In addition to this, I had the time of my life. It is no wonder that old men send young men to war. Old men, who have survived, tend to remember the good times, the adventure and the independence. It is hard to remember the fear and the pain.

But I had outsmarted myself. Instead of getting into the action I wanted, I remained in London, while our troops and the troops of our Allies stormed the beaches of Normandy on June 6, 1944.

It became apparent to me that my colonel had intended to use me as his personal interpreter when he and the rest of the general staff moved to France. My colonel knew the date of the invasion – the technical term was he was witting - but first, France had to be liberated, and I sat in London not doing anything about it.

While our troops were heroically engaged in that task, I spent my days and nights in the comfort of London.

This comfort was interrupted slightly by the German V-1 and V-2 rockets.

London was still under blackout regulations. In fact, if you wandered around Soho in the hours of darkness, you would frequently feel a gentle hand gliding over your arm and shoulder to determine your rank, and a seductive voice offering you the delights of heaven for a fee appropriate to that rank. In view of the abundance of volunteers, I wonder how these ladies ever made any money.

Air raids by the Luftwaffe were few and far between. However, the rockets started to come, and there was no defense against them. By the time the air raid sirens had sounded, the rockets had exploded. There was no point to sounding the sirens or going into shelters. You heard the motors of the rockets – a very distinctive sound, the first jet engines I had ever heard. Then the motor stopped.

Sometimes, the rocket would go into a glide and explode a distance away; sometimes it would fall straight down.

I remember once, standing in a store near Piccadilly surrounded by glass on all sides, when the motor of one of the rockets stopped. I remember thinking what all that glass would do to me if the rocket landed nearby. Fortunately it didn't.

The V-1 and V-2 rockets merely increased the hectic atmosphere in London, the attitude of live today for tomorrow we may die.

For a long time after the invasion, our forces were held to the beaches of Normandy. During that time, enormous quantities of equipment were delivered to the small, liberated area of France.

Now it was time for us to go to France. A small snag developed. I had never fired my rifle. Remember, I only had three weeks of basic training instead of twelve, before being transferred to Camp Ritchie. I could fieldstrip the rifle, clean it and reassemble it, but I had no idea about shooting it.

According to army regulations, I could not go into a combat zone without having fired my rifle, and the record of my doing so would have to show in my service papers.

One afternoon, I went to a firing range in Brighton, an hour away. Quickly I was taught how to fire from a standing position, kneeling and from a prone position. I fired for the record, - and miraculously did well enough to qualify for a sharpshooter's medal, the lowest of the three kinds of medals to be awarded.

It was now August. Most of Normandy was in our hands. There had been an invasion of Southern France by our Seventh Army, aided by French troops under General de Lattre de Tassigny.

Suddenly, there was a breakout. In a major battle, our troops broke through the German forces keeping them inside Normandy, defeated and captured large numbers of Germans, and led by General Patton's tanks raced toward Paris.

My colonel and several generals above him, finally decided to join the war, and I went with them.

CHAPTER 14

We got on a plane – the second flight of my life, and this time I fervently hoped to be allowed to walk down the stairs of the plane. We flew to Cherbourg, the main port in Normandy. There was still fighting in the area. We had to turn back and delay our landing.

We finally landed and all the officers went off to find accommodations. As the sole enlisted man on the plane, it was of course my duty to stay behind and guard their luggage.

Suddenly, it turned out that I was badly needed. All the highly trained Camp Ritchie graduates were in replacement depots back in England; I was in France.

The Supreme Command had decided to allow the French the honor of liberating Paris, but a French speaking American was needed to liaison with the headquarters of General de Lattre de Tassigny, and to be among the first to enter Paris with the tank division of General Leclerc. That American turned out to be me.

When the Army wants to, it can move fast. Instantly, I was commissioned a Special Agent of the Counter Intelligence Corps. I was given officer's uniform without insignia of rank, and told to introduce myself as Mr. Lerner from the War Department. If anyone asked my rank, I was instructed to say: "My rank is confidential, but I am not outranked presently." In this manner, I could deal with officers of much higher rank.

My real rank depended on the speed with which the army completed its paperwork.

I said a grateful farewell to my colonel. He was gracious enough to wish me good luck, although I am sure that he regretted the loss of his personal interpreter.

I got into another, very small plane and was taken to an airfield South of Paris, and from there by jeep to the headquarters of the Free French Forces.

This was my first time in a jeep in a combat zone. I was aware of the fact that regulations required that the windshield had to be lowered and that weapons had to be in firing position as we drove, but I did not know why there was a metal post attached to the front of the vehicle. My driver explained that the retreating Germans had the unpleasant habit of placing wires across the roads, and that several injuries and even decapitations resulted from that. The metal post was the solution to that problem.

On August 25th 1944, the French entered Paris and I was with them. There was still sniper fire. Some German troops had holed up here and there, and there had been quite a bit of fighting between the French underground forces – called the FFI – the Forces Francaises de l'Interieur – and some German troops, but by the time we moved in, the jubilation of the population was such that no one paid any attention to that.

I spent only a few days attached to the staff of General Leclerc, but because I was there, later on they handed out some medals and gave me the Croix de Guerre. It was totally undeserved; I was just along for the ride.

The moment I arrived in Paris, my job was changed once more. Again, the demand for people with my skills had not been properly anticipated.

On the Avenue Foch, one of the most elegant streets of Paris, not far from the Arc de Triomphe, stood the Palais Rothschild, a beautiful nineteenth century building with a large interior courtyard. It had of course been the home of the famous banking family, and because the Rothschild's were Jewish, it had immediately been confiscated by the German occupation troops. The Gestapo, the German Secret police, had made it its headquarters.

I found myself in that building with three other CIC agents who had been located. In a manner that could only be described as vengeful, the FFI arrested civilians by the hundreds; some were German soldiers who had put on mufti and tried to disappear among the general population, some were French collaborators or members of the Milice, some officials of the French puppet government, and many, innocent victims of their neighbors.

All these detainees were herded into the courtyard. It was my task and that of my three fellow CIC agents to sort out these people, release the innocent and direct the others into appropriate channels for further investigation.

I found a bed in the Grand Palais, an exhibition hall on the Champs Elysees, which was filled with cots supplied by our quartermaster corps. After a few days, I moved into a hotel near the Gare du Nord. I was far more independent now that I was an officer.

Following are some photos that deserve an explanation: As a CIC Special Agent, I was given a badge, a special ID and three hand weapons: A .45 Colt, a German Walther, which I used when I wore civilian clothes because it was flat and could easily be concealed, and a small .38 Colt revolver, which I wore on my belt most of the time because it was very light.

Of course, I had never fired any of these guns, not even for practice.

This is a photo of me in officer's uniform.

Wasn't I young and handsome then?

And there is a photo with a German cap that was used to provide me with German ID for one particular mission later on.

And finally, there is my driver's license. I had never driven a car in my life, but one of my teammates taught me how to drive a jeep, and another teammate issued the driver's license. Officers could do that for each other.

Driver's license

Back to Paris and the Palais Rothschild:

One of the arrestees I released was a Russian émigré who had fled the revolution in 1917, and who owned a nightclub near Place Pigalle. Of course, Germans and their French companions frequented his nightclub, but that did not make him a collaborator in my eyes. In 1947, when I was in Paris on business, I happened to walk past his nightclub. He recognized me and invited me to spend the evening at his expense.

Another man I released was a typical upper class Frenchman, a retired colonial officer, who had had nothing to do with the Germans, but whose haughty manner had antagonized the concierge in his building. After interviewing this functionary, I came to the conclusion that the only thing the prisoner could be accused of was the arrogance of his class (including, I am sure, an inborn anti-Semitism).

After I released him, he showed up bringing me as gifts a German sword and a German helmet, which had been in his family from the previous German occupation of Paris in 1871.

There were also a number of young women whose offense had been that they had slept with German soldiers. Their friends and neighbors had punished them by shaving their heads. Once we established that their former lovers had not been people of importance, we let them go. They had been punished enough. I wonder whether any of the people who were so judgmental with them, had ever had any business dealings with the German occupiers.

And for the first time, I confronted a high-ranking SS Officer, a Sturmbannfuehrer (Major), whose escape from Paris had been frustrated by the FFI. When I saw him standing before me, a tremendous wave of hatred swept over me. He represented all the evil that he and his kind had brought into the world. And now, he was in my hands to do with as I pleased.

But if I did my job right, he could provide me with some very useful information and, I hoped, would ultimately be punished for his crimes by competent authority. So, I made a major effort to control myself, and began my interrogation with complete courtesy.

The French could not do enough for us as their liberators. People would come up to me on the street and invite me to dinner, or just shake my hand or – in the case of young women particularly – hug me and thank me as if I had been personally responsible for liberating France from the Nazis.

A few days after the liberation of Paris, there was a major parade down the Champs Elysees, starting at the Arc de Triomphe, led by General de Gaulle. I participated in that parade.

But trust the French. In late November, when our advance had stalled at the German border, - before the Battle of the Bulge- I was in Paris on a three day pass. As I wandered the city, I heard nothing but bitter complaints against the "American Occupation". There was not enough food, not enough coal, not enough electricity, and all of it was the Americans' fault.

The fact that the war was far from over was totally ignored by the complainers.

But before I could get too angry at the French, I went to the Comedie Francaise and was given a ticket for that night's performance of Moliere's Tartuffe. I paid my respects to the chair Moliere sat in when he died on stage during a performance, and I marveled at his courage in writing plays that attacked the hypocrisies of his time.

Back to the liberation of Paris:

I spent about three weeks there. By that time the Army got things organized a little better as far as my fate was concerned. I was assigned to a team of six CIC agents attached to Twelfth Army Group Headquarters. The Twelfth Army Group, commanded by General Omar Bradley, comprised the First Army, under General Hodges, the Third Army, commanded by General Patton, the Seventh Army that had landed in St. Tropez in the South of France, as well as a number of other units, including some of our Allies.

Not all the jeeps available to us had been equipped with the metal posts that would protect us against the wire retreating Germans or their Collaborationist Allies liked to place across the roads. There was a lot of competition and pulling of rank to obtain properly equipped jeeps, but that is the Army way.

I got acquainted with my team and found that most of them had been law enforcement officers, and that only two of them spoke German, no other member of the team spoke French. Their job, it seems had indeed been Counter Intelligence – looking for spies in the United States. They were somewhat lost as to what they would do in France. Apparently I was the only one to have some ideas, because of my Camp Ritchie training. I did not mention my involvement with the OSS. I just wondered whether I would ever hear from that organization again.

We travelled to Verdun in Eastern France, the scene of one of the greatest and most murderous battles of World War I. Twelfth Army Group Headquarters was in a huge caserne – barracks – dating from World War 1.

After we got settled, I took a little walk outside the barracks. Small attached houses lined the street.

I got into a conversation with a middle-aged man standing in front of his home. Astonished that he could talk to me in French, he invited me in, and asked his wife quickly to make an apple pie. I never saw one made so quickly, nor have I ever tasted one better.

My friend said that the German occupiers always behaved correctly, but that there were always shortages of food. Apparently there was a hospital attached to the caserne, where my friend worked as an orderly. He also told me that there were German soldiers being cared for in that hospital.

Upon my return to the caserne, I checked and found that no one had bothered looking at the patients and that many of them indeed were German soldiers abandoned by their companions during their retreat.

After a few days, we took over an old jail near the center of the small town of Verdun. The jail had been used by the Gestapo, and now it became our home. We each took a cell and fixed it up as well as possible. We had an attachment of MP's assigned to us, and were expecting some high-ranking prisoners to occupy the other cells. Then our interrogations could begin. Two Free French Officers also were attached to the team.

I spent about five months in Verdun. From there I went out on a number of missions for the OSS. Yes, indeed, they called upon me. As I indicated before, I cannot go into details, but I will tell some of the more amusing incidents.

There is one point I would like to emphasize. During the three years it took from leaving Vienna until my family and I landed in the

United States, we felt powerless. We were literally without a country, exposed to being abused by all with no one to defend us. Once I became an American citizen and an American soldier, I knew that I had the entire might of the United States with me. Even when I was alone in enemy territory, I was not alone, because I was an American.

Back to my adventures:

As it turns out, even if I wanted to, I could not tell much. In most cases, I went to a certain location, met a certain person, exchanged some materials and got back as soon as possible. Sometimes I wore civilian clothes and sometimes uniform. I did not know what the materials were, nor whom I interacted with. That was strictly determined by tradecraft.

During my stay in Verdun, one of my teammates, volunteered to teach me how to drive. Within a few weeks, I drove a jeep with the best of them, stick shift and all.

In Verdun I had occasion to visit the battlefield and the cemetery. I do not know how many hundreds of thousands men died during that battle in World War I, but it was a horrifying number.

Now I will tell you of the most dangerous mission I had to undertake:

We had captured a German Colonel and his two civilian secretaries, two charming young women. The Colonel was most cooperative and we got a lot of good information from him. We kept the secretaries in our jail, even though they were civilians, because they, too, had a great deal of useful information they were eager to share.

Then one of the girls embarrassed me greatly, by telling me that her period was approaching and that she desperately needed sanitary napkins. It now became my task to find those crucial supplies.

Remember, this was 1944 – the dark, almost Victorian age as far as you liberated young people are concerned, and I was very young.

There was a WAC (Women's Army Corps) detachment at headquarters. With my newly acquired driving skills, I drove twenty miles to the rear, to the Army Barracks occupied by Twelfth Army Group. I mounted stairs to a Hall, that in retrospect seems to me to have been the size of a football field. It was filled with what seemed to be hundreds of nubile young American women, all working busily at typewriters. At the far end of the Hall, there was the desk of the WAC Major, who, in my recollection looked very much like the wicked witch of the West. She shouted across the heads of all those lovely American girls: "What do you want?"

The clatter of the typewriters ceased and all the girls looked at me. I asked for permission to approach the dragon lady to explain my mission to her.

She refused. "What do you want?" She repeated.

Finally, I shouted across the heads of all the WACS looking at me: " I need some Kotex."

Dead silence. Finally, I was permitted to approach the presence so that I could explain my predicament. The WAC Major informed me that there was a PX in a supply depot another twenty miles to the rear, and that it had a special section for WACS. She gave me a note to the Quartermaster, allowing me to draw "female equipment."

I shot out of there, hearing the giggles of all those delightful young women.

At the PX, I had to convince the Quartermaster that I was not looking for Kotex for my French girlfriend. Even the note from the WAC Major was not enough. Finally, I had to pull rank, and show my CIC identification.

I finally returned to Verdun with my mission successfully accomplished, but at the price of considerable embarrassment.

And then I was arrested.

CHAPTER 15

The war on our front had again become somewhat of a stalemate. We had liberated France, but the Germans had major fortifications – the Siegfried Line – at their border, and they had the protection of the Rhine. We were not ready to attack in the winter. In the meantime, the Russians continued to advance on the Eastern Front.

In the Intelligence Community, from our interrogations of captured soldiers, we had information of major troop movements to our front. Some of us felt that these movements were not only for defensive purposes, but our commanders discounted the possibility of the Germans mounting a counter offensive in the winter.

Allied Armies had occupied the Southern half of Italy. There had been a palace revolution. Mussolini was overthrown, and Italy switched sides, and became a co-belligerent (not an Ally) against Germany.

Mussolini was arrested and housed in a mountain lodge. German paratroopers led by SS Obersturmbannfuehrer Otto von Skorzeny rescued him in a daring mission. Mussolini was taken to Germany and then resumed command as a German puppet of the section of Italy still occupied by German troops.

Skorzeny was Hitler's favorite commando. His rank in the Waffen SS – the four divisions the SS Paramilitary Organization mounted – was the equivalent of Lieutenant Colonel. He had been born in Vienna and had joined the Austrian Nazi Party as early as 1930. He was a fanatic Nazi, but also the picture of an authentic German war hero, tall, handsome, scar faced, and an excellent, fearless soldier.

After my Kotex adventure, I was sent to Metz. There had been a jeep accident, involving two soldiers. One was dead, the other badly injured. The papers the two men carried aroused suspicion

They were more than suspicious. I found that the dog tags of one of the men showed the letter H for Hebrew, but that the man was not circumcised and so there was a reasonable presumption that he was not Jewish.

The man was badly injured, but his wounds had been treated by our doctors and he was lucid enough to be able to answer questions.

Apparently, he and his partner were part of a group who had been sent across the lines in American uniforms. The organizer and commander of this attempt was Skorzeny. What their ultimate mission was, I could not determine.

In the meantime, however, we had heard from other sources, that Skorzeny had organized teams of English speaking soldiers, equipped with captured American uniforms and jeeps, and that their mission was to assassinate as many high ranking members of the Allied High Command, starting with General Eisenhower, as possible.

What I found in Metz confirmed this information.

It was immediately disseminated throughout the Allied forces, with extra security in place for the commanders and precautions on all roads.

On my way back to Verdun from Metz, I was stopped by a patrol and arrested. Ah, my accent.

In war movies they always check the bona fides of a suspect by asking him about the Dodgers or the Yankees. That wouldn't have helped me then, nor would it help me today.

It took several hours in the headquarters of a very suspicious front-line colonel until he was persuaded that I was indeed who I said I was, and that I was released.

A few days later, I left Verdun and drove to Luxembourg City for a meeting with other CIC personnel. Everything was quiet, except for what we thought was a desperation measure, these assassination teams. We wanted to discuss how best to cope with them.

And then, all hell broke loose. Field Marshall von Rundstedt, at 70 still the commander of the Western front, launched his offensive, which later was known as the Battle of the Bulge. The attack was later considered a total failure of intelligence on our part. I do not share that view. I think we had all the information we could ever expect to obtain. Our failure was to draw the proper conclusions and to act upon them.

German tanks sliced through our lines with the aim of reaching the North Sea and cutting the Allied positions in half. If the assassination teams had succeeded, the lack of proper command positions could have aggravated our situation seriously.

If Rundstedt had reached the Sea, this would have been a major setback and certainly would have prolonged the war.

Of course, I did not know what was going on. When you are on the ground, you do not get much of a strategic overview.

All I knew was that suddenly there was artillery fire all around us. We were told that there was an attack, and that our position in Northern Luxembourg was almost completely surrounded. We had been far away from the front, but suddenly, the front had advanced to our location.

All personnel, cooks and bakers, typists and supply clerks, and CIC agents, were required for defense.

I spent the next three days and nights in the trenches in the snow. By that time, I did not have my M-1 rifle any more. Instead, I carried a carbine, a lighter and smaller version of the M-1, an officer's weapon. I also had a Colt .45 pistol on my belt. I had never fired either of these guns.

During the three days and nights, I had occasion to fire the carbine a great deal. We had spotters in foxholes several hundred yards ahead of our positions. Every once in a while, word came down that there was an attack, and we were given the order to shoot.

It was snowing a lot and it was generally very overcast when it was not snowing. I never saw any one attacking, nor did I see any enemy when I fired, but when the order was given to shoot, I shot.

It was cold and wet, but somehow that did not bother us that much. I think we had other worries.

After three days, the weather cleared and our air force came onto the scene. The German attack was blunted and after constant attacks by our air force and ground troops, within a couple of weeks the Battle of the Bulge was over.

As for me, after the three days, I was relieved of my duties on the line, spent a few days in Luxembourg City and then returned to Verdun.

This was my only time in combat, and I never saw the enemy during that time.

Shortly after my return to Verdun, I was sent by my handler to a meeting in a church. I was in civilian clothes standing in the rear of the church while a Service was going on. I looked for the person I was to meet, when I felt a pull on my sleeve. A little old lady held up her Psalter and offered very kindly to share it with me. I spent the rest of the service belting out the psalms as well as I could, although I was always a beat behind the nice old lady. At the end of the service, I thanked her and went off to try to find my counterpart.

When spring came, we attacked. The Germans blew up all the bridges over the Rhine, but failed to do so with the bridge at Remagen.

Not far from Remagen, at Oppenheim, the terrain was suitable for pontoon bridges and material was brought up to construct them.

The Remagen bridge had been damaged in the attempt to blow it up, but was strong enough for some of our troops and equipment to cross. This was the first crossing of the Rhine into the heartland of Germany.

The Germans sent two Frog Men to destroy the bridge. It is almost impossible to defend against a well-trained and well-equipped scuba diver, unless you have plenty of time to install protective netting and other devices. However, fate was with us. One diver's oxygen tank got entangled in some of the spear like protuberances left from the original attempt to blow up the bridge.

The diver's companion attempted to liberate him, and an observant American soldier gave the alarm.

The two frog men were brought to us for interrogation. We found that their training to use the SCUBA gear had taken place in the Dianabad in Vienna, a large indoor pool complex I had visited many times. My familiarity with that place was very helpful in the process of persuading the prisoners to reveal what we needed to know.

Apparently, there was another group of divers preparing to blow up the pontoon bridge at Oppenheim as soon as our engineers had completed it.

This could have been a disaster. Imagine a bridge filled with American personnel, tanks and trucks, exploding.

We decided that it was important to stop this attempt.

Three of our combat trained MP's volunteered to go along. They were equipped with B.A.R.s (Browning Automatic Rifles) and hand grenades.

I put on the uniform of a German officer, obtained from the hospital. We took a boat across the Rhine well upstream from the fighting that was going on near the bridges. It was dark, and we rowed as quietly as possible (I finally found out what it means to muffle oars). I began to realize my folly in volunteering for this mission. I remember that there was a lot of light from the moon, but that a cloud covered it as we began rowing.

Our troops along the Rhine were supposed to have been instructed not to fire on us, and we fervently hoped that every American soldier within a fifty mile radius had gotten the word.

The intent was, that if we were spotted, I would stand up in my German uniform and try to bluff that I was a German officer escorting three American prisoners of war. This would not work under close scrutiny, but might avoid our getting shot while we were crossing the river.

Fortunately, I never had to test this plan. We crossed the Rhine without being spotted, and were able to make our way down to the camp of the swimmers. Our principal aim was to destroy the oxygen equipment used by the SCUBA divers and we knew where it was stored.

My three companions let loose their guns and threw their hand grenades. This took just a few seconds. We did not wait to see the results, but withdrew – actually ran as quickly as possible, to a nearby barn we had spotted. We holed up in the loft of the barn for two days, until we saw American troops going past.

Then it was up to my companions to explain that I was not really a German officer, and we were able to return to my unit.

I do not know whether we killed any of the Frog Men, but we must have eliminated their oxygen tanks.

The Remagen bridge collapsed ten days after our troops crossed. Scuba divers never attacked three Pontoon bridges at Oppenheim and Patton's Third Army crossed the Rhine on them.

The war was going well.

Hitler had committed suicide, the Russians occupied Berlin, and Germany surrendered unconditionally on May 8, 1945. The war in Europe was over.

We went into Bavaria. Now our mission changed. The OSS halted its operations, and by September 1945 was disbanded. It would be another two years before the Central Intelligence Agency was created, originally out of the remnants of the OSS.

Our mission as Counter Intelligence Agents was two-fold. There was supposed to be a German resistance organization, called the Werewolves, hidden in the Mountains of Southern Germany. Even if it existed, we never found any Germans involved in a resistance effort. The surrender was total.

And our other, and if I may say so, our principal mission, was to find and arrest Nazis. This was not as easy as it sounds; they had all disappeared from the face of the earth. No one was or had ever been a Nazi, even the original members of the Nazi party.

We had a booklet, the size of a paper back, issued by SHAEF (Supreme Headquarters Allied Expeditionary Force). It listed all positions in the German Government and in its various paramilitary organizations that were subject to automatic arrest and investigation. In addition, all members of the SS were subject to automatic arrest. The entire SS was declared a criminal organization.

The SS (Schutz Staffel) (Protective Unit) had been created by Heinrich Himmler, and under him grew to be a separate army. It controlled all German Intelligence Activities, the SD (Sicherheits Dienst) , the GESTAPO (Geheime Staats Polizei) (Secret State Police), all Concentration Camps – they were all manned by SS personnel, and four fully equipped combat divisions (the Waffen SS).

At least in one respect, they made our task easier. All SS personnel, without exception, had their blood group tattooed near their left armpit. So, when we found a suspect, it was easy enough to determine whether such a tattoo existed or whether there had been an attempt to remove it.

We too, had our blood groups with us. They were marked on our dog tags.

We were assigned an area called Kreis Crailsheim, in Bavaria. There was no more resistance even though the surrender had not been announced as yet. We drove first to Augsburg and then to Munich. On the way to Munich, we stopped at the concentration camp of Dachau.

Dachau is a suburb of Munich and the home of the very first of Germany's concentration camps.

The first American troops had reached Dachau just two days earlier. Even though Dachau was not an extermination camp like Auschwitz, there were still bodies of inmates scattered about, some of whom had died from starvation or abuse by their guards. Other inmates in their striped pajamas were on the verge of dying of malnutrition and disease. When our troops arrived and saw the starving prisoners, they gave them food. Unfortunately, in a number of cases, the inmates died from eating too much and too fast.

The fleeing guards had not taken the time to clean up and there were bones lying about near the crematorium.

These two photos are what we saw in Dachau-the bodies and bones of those who had been murdered.

I will never forget the smells and sights of that unholy place.

Munich was very badly destroyed. It had been the capital of the Nazi movement. Hitler's first attempt to take power had taken place there. The official headquarters of the Nazi party was the Brown House in central Munich.

It took me two hours of searching through the rubble to find the ruins of the Brown House, and I took some satisfaction in having a picture taken of me standing on its rubble.

The heroic pose: I stand on the ruins of the Brown House.

My team at the entrance of the Camp.

Photographs of some of the horrors found in the Camps were exhibited in store windows throughout Germany on orders from SHAEF under the title: "Diese Greueltaten sind Eure Schuld". Those horrible deeds are your fault.

CHAPTER 16

Kreis Crailsheim was a bucolic area in the mountains, seemingly untouched by the war, dominated by a Schloss owned by the local baron. I went in, and in typical conqueror's fashion, gave the baron and his wife one hour to get out and to turn over the Schloss to us. He found quarters in the village, and for the next six weeks, we enjoyed living in baronial splendor, served by the baron's staff and fawned upon by the villagers.

Was the baron a Nazi? Probably not. He had been a high-ranking officer in World War I and was too old to serve in the military during World War II. But in my mind, he was as responsible for the actions of the German Government as any German, in fact, more so because of his high position in German society.

The automatic arrest list did not include military personnel deemed to have done their duty as soldiers, although the highest ranks were given special scrutiny in the denazification process. They may have commanded areas in which atrocities were committed and they would have to share the responsibility for them.

In addition, I had the authority to arrest any one else whose face I did not like. People we arrested were first sent to reception camps where they were interrogated and either released or kept for further investigation.

To demonstrate our contempt for the vanquished Germans, SHAEF had ordered a non-fraternization policy. Since I had to interact with Germans in my duties, I was exempt from its regulations, but Germans like to shake hands, and I went through all kinds of maneuvers to avoid shaking a German hand.

How long the non-fraternization policy lasted when it came to our soldiers and the German girls eagerly looking for any one who could supply them with food in exchange for their favors, I leave it up to you to judge.

I met and dealt with many very high ranking officials, party members and SS Officers, but none of them had accepted the Nazi ideology. They had all been forced to go along on pain of death, but in their heart of hearts they were opposed to Nazism and were true democrats, and above all, they loved Jews.

And they also believed in the Easter Bunny!

The automatic arrest booklet became my Bible. In Crailsheim I devised a questionnaire, had it printed by the local printer and distributed by the mayors of all the villages. With typical German efficiency, they brought back thousands of properly filled out replies. After that, it was easy to arrest those who deserved it and I sent truckloads to the nearest reception center.

One of the castles in the area was owned and occupied by a cousin of the King of England. The Windsors are a German family after all. He had been a colonel in the NSKK – the National Socialist Kraftfahrer Korps – the Automobile Club, essentially, but like all German organizations, built on military lines.

As such, he had strutted in many parades and had supported the Nazis with his name and title.

It gave me a considerable amount of pleasure to arrest him, but three days later, he was back in residence, fully denazified.

It pays to have connections.

In addition to checking the questionnaires, we conducted raids on the villages from time to time. It was a busy and satisfying time. I enjoyed hunting Nazis and sending them off for further investigation.

After six weeks in Crailsheim, we were transferred to Wiesbaden, where I spent the balance of my military career.

Wiesbaden is an attractive mid-size city at the foot of the Taunus Mountains. There were few signs of the war, here and there a few buildings gone or partly damaged, but nothing like Munich or Frankfurt, which had largely been leveled.

We took over the luxurious home of a banker in the most prestigious section of town. It is nice to be a conqueror. Here we had the banker's servants and great accommodations.

It took many years and much effort in my civilian life, before I lived with as many creature comforts.

In the center of town, there was a lovely park with a Kurhaus – a building used for restaurants, concerts and shows. This was taken over by the American Red Cross and became a source of entertainment and relaxation for the many American troops in the area.

In the mountains outside of town, there was a beautiful outdoor swimming pool, the Opel Bad, founded by the Opel automobile concern. This was reserved only for the use of American soldiers. I used it frequently that summer.

Once, a troupe of French entertainers came to town to perform for the troops, and their girls appeared at the pool in scandalous two-piece bathing suits to the great joy of all attendees. That day, I was very happy to be able to speak French.

The rest of the time, the pool was mostly a male preserve. There were not many WACS around.

We created a great deal of publicity asking the civilian population to help us find the criminals, who were responsible for their suffering.

Then we opened a CIC office in a storefront, in anticipation of having a lot of walk-in traffic of people denouncing their neighbors. And they came. It was quite a job to sort out who the real Nazis were. There were times when the denouncer was arrested together with his victim.

My own job, however, was not in that office. I took over the criminal police and had an office in the Police Commissariat.

I also acquired a secretary, a seventeen-year-old girl named Erika Muller. She developed a crush on me, but I did not take advantage, partly because of her age, but principally because she was German. I simply could not be too friendly with any German, and I had to work very hard to be polite and correct with the German policemen whom I supervised.

Erika had an older sister who worked for one of my teammates, who was not as scrupulous.

In addition to the police, I was responsible for the municipal jail. Many arrestees from the area were housed there until there was transport.

Among the most prominent guests in my jail, was Julius Streicher, the editor and owner of the Nazi paper "Der Stuermer", and one of leading anti-Semites in a country of anti-Semites. His publication was filled with scurrilous stories about Jews. On the bottom of the front page of his newspaper, in big black letter, was always the phrase: " Die Juden sind unser Unglueck." The Jews are our misfortune.

He had also been Gauleiter (Governor) of the province of Franconia. He was tried and convicted at Nuremberg and executed a year after he enjoyed my hospitality.

It took a great deal of restraint to treat him like any other prisoner, but I made sure that he and others I arrested knew that I was a Jew.

It was the intention of the Allies to demonstrate to the German people that their actions had put them beyond the pale of the community of nations.

Military Government (MG) engaged in a propaganda campaign to show the German people what they had done. In addition to the photos in store windows of concentration camp atrocities, mentioned before, there were group tours organized with the most prominent citizens, the doctors, lawyers, University professors, bankers and so forth. These tours were taken to the nearest concentration camp and to Displaced Persons' Camps where these good citizens could listen to stories by the victims.

It was interesting to watch people stop and look at the exhibits in the store windows, and at times I stood there – in civilian clothes- listening to the reactions.

There was a DP (Displaced Persons) Camp outside of town, filled with the flotsam of war – former prisoners of war mostly from the East, who did not want to go back to Soviet-dominated Europe, former slave laborers, former members of German organized Foreign Legions who, rightly, were afraid to go back home, and of course survivors of concentration camps.

I spent a lot of time there, even though this was not part of my regular duties, to try and help any Jews I could find. Many attempted to go to the United States, and my familiarity with the documentary hurdles that had to be overcome was very useful.

Among those, there were a mother and daughter, tattooed with their concentration camp numbers, and I was able to help them with their paper work.

Two years later, at City College in New York, I met the daughter in class.

Some of these camps remained in existence for years. Many of the liberated survivors eventually made it to the United States. Others followed an organized, illegal route to the British Mandate of Palestine. Some of those who were caught on that route were interned by the British in Cyprus.

Of course after Israel achieved independence the gates were open and there was a flood of survivors from Europe who entered the Jewish state.

In the fall of 1945 I got a one-week pass. I gave serious consideration to going to Vienna and showing up there as an American Officer with a gun at my hip, but I soon decided that nothing good would come of such a visit.

Instead, I went to London, visited Tante Regina and Monica, and lived as a civilian for a few days.

There were a few interesting incidents in Wiesbaden:

Cars were freely available to us, as conquerors. Every time we found and arrested a high-ranking Nazi, we confiscated his Mercedes. Every time I got a Mercedes to replace my jeep, some higher-ranking officer took it away from me. Finally, I confiscated a small two-seater BMW, and that remained my car until I went home.

I conducted raids in various locations, using the German police. I thought it was very revealing of the German character how enthusiastic they were in finding and arresting their compatriots. Charitably, I could attribute this to the fact that the people who had been in high positions in the Nazi regime had lorded it over their fellow citizens, who now took their revenge.

Let me explain that I was very much aware of the fact that in most cases, people subject to automatic arrest according to the SHAEF guidelines would spend only a few months in our detention centers and then be released, unless there was real evidence of war crimes. Nevertheless, I felt that even such a short period was salutary and well deserved.

Once, after conducting a raid on Biebrich, a suburb of Wiesbaden, I received an anonymous letter address to the "Hangman of Biebrich" warning me of dire consequences if I did not cease my pursuit of German patriots. But there was really no German resistance to the occupation.

Periodically, rumors would intensify about the Werewolves. And there was always Skorzeny, who was supposed to lead them and who would emerge from the mountains to inflict damage on Allied troops. But they were only rumors.

Nevertheless, finding Skorzeny became a priority. It was not that he was a war criminal, he really was not. He was a brave and fanatic soldier. But we wanted to be sure that he did not continue a war that was over.

Hitler had made much of the "Alpine Redoubt", an area in Bavaria and Austria in the mountains that supposedly would be prepared to fight on forever, equipped with all kinds of armaments and major underground fortifications. We could never find any traces of it.

But we thought Skorzeny was just the man who would know about this.

Finally, he showed up. He was found as an ordinary prisoner of war in a PW camp. He spoke freely of his exploits and of all the plans for the Alpine Redoubt. As it happens, these plans were hatched in the Propaganda Ministry, but never realized.

Skorzeny was tried for sending the assassination teams across the lines, and was found not guilty. What he had done was what a good soldier in wartime should do. And was it so different from what we had done?

After his release, Skorzeny moved to Spain. He showed up later on as an adviser to Egypt and Syria in their wars against the new state of Israel. His anti-Semitism continued to guide his behavior.

CHAPTER 17

In the fall of 1945, in a hall with a damaged roof, Jewish High Holiday services took place. An Army Chaplain – a Rabbi - conducted the services. Most of the congregation consisted of Jewish soldiers of all ranks, but there were also quite a few Jews who had survived the Nazi onslaught and emerged from DP camps to show up.

I listened to Kol Nidre, the prayer that begins the holiest day of the year, the Day of Atonement. I was wearing my uniform and had my .45 Colt at my belt – and I looked around at the congregation of Jews in defeated Germany, and I was very proud.

There is not a day of my life that I have not been grateful for having been born a Jew and for being able to share in the history and values of our people.

Later that fall, there was the first post-war performance of an opera in Wiesbaden in the same hall. Because the roof was damaged and it was a cold evening, the audience wore coats. One of the singers was an informant of mine, and so I attended. It was Madama Butterfly – and it was lovely.

I wore civilian clothes on several occasions. This time it was far less hazardous than while the fighting was still going on.

One time I was supposed to meet an anonymous informant in a Catholic church during mass. The informant did not show up and my time was wasted.

Another time, I bugged the living room of a high-class prostitute whose clientele was supposed to include some wanted people. Again, this was a fruitless endeavor; the clients she expected never showed up, and after three days, we abandoned that effort.

This is symptomatic of a lot of intelligence work. A great deal of time is wasted, but every once in a while there is a nugget – if you recognize it – which makes the effort worthwhile.

One day, one of my teammates and I, aided by the German Police, conducted one of our raids. We surrounded an apartment building and went from apartment to apartment starting at the top floor and working our way down, checking on the identities of the people we found.

In one apartment, I started to question a man who claimed to have been an ordinary soldier, but who said he had lost his Soldbuch – the Pay Book which every soldier carried, and which listed every place he had been stationed and every unit he had been assigned to. For us, checking the Soldbuch often provided very useful information.

I ordered the man to raise his shirt, and there was the telltale SS Tattoo under his left armpit. I told him that he would have to come with us. He asked for permission to get his jacket from his bedroom in the back.

He emerged from the bedroom swinging a rubber truncheon at me. I pulled out my revolver, closed my eyes, remembered that there was no bullet in the chamber and so squeezed the trigger twice. The bullet hit him and broke his arm.

I had never fired the revolver before. I am sure that if I had not closed my eyes I would not have hit him. My reaction was one of sheer panic, when I saw him running at me with the truncheon.

This was a very fortunate shot, because he could have struck me with the truncheon even if I had hit him elsewhere. The revolver does not have much stopping power. I was extremely lucky.

We took our prisoner to a military hospital where he was treated before being sent onward for investigation and prosecution.

After this, I kept the truncheon on my desk and often played with it while questioning recalcitrant customers. It is interesting how quickly they answered questions when they observed me doing that.

I have brought the truncheon home, and it is among my more valued souvenirs.

There was an ammunition depot near Wiesbaden. I was driving near it one day, when there was a major explosion. Suddenly I was surrounded by screaming civilians accusing me, as an American soldier, for the damage and mayhem. I got very nervous, and started to wave my gun about, but except for screaming at me, nobody made a hostile move.

I went into the ammunition depot and saw a great deal of damage and several civilians and soldiers dead and wounded.

We spent a lot of time investigating the explosion, but could find no trace of sabotage. Our conclusion was that it was an accident, with some kind of spontaneous combustion as its cause.

After the defeat of Germany, the next task was the defeat of Japan. There were rumors of troop transfers to the Pacific Theater of War, and in fact, some units were embarked to destinations unknown.   But in August we dropped two atomic bombs on Japan.   Japan surrendered. The war was over!

CHAPTER 18

By fall the Army had set up a system of getting the troops home for demobilization. This was a point system, with so many points for each month served, with extra points for service overseas, and extra points for serving in a combat zone.

It appeared that out of the five official battles listed in the European Theater of Operations, I had been in four, missing out on the invasion of Normandy (my ETO medal carries four battle stars). It became clear that I would be able to go home by early winter.

I was approached by higher authority and asked to re-enlist for at least one year. I would be promoted and transferred to Military Government. My skills and languages were badly needed. "Just think of all the good you can do!" Higher Authority urged.

I had a tremendous amount of power, and I lived very comfortably. But I was only twenty-one, and I thought that it was time to start my own life. Nevertheless, I gave the matter a great deal of thought.

Then Military Government needed a fire chief for the city of Wiesbaden. They picked an experienced man and sent him to me for vetting. I arrested him on the spot.

MG found another candidate and sent him to me. I arrested him as well.

They sent me a third potential fire chief. He, too, was subject to automatic arrest according to the SHAEF guidelines.

I had an excited call from the head of military government, who outranked me by several steps. He explained that you had to be experienced to run the Fire Department of a large city like Wiesbaden.

I responded, pointing out that the Fire Department was run like a Para-military organization by the Nazis, and that all three of his candidates had held ranks subject to automatic arrest.

"But where can I find a Fire Chief?" he asked. I had no answer for him.

He asked me to pick the least offensive of the three. I refused. I went by the book. If SHAEF wanted to change the automatic arrest categories, let them do so, and let them call me from Headquarters in Frankfurt.

And indeed they did. As I knew they would. I was overruled. And I knew that denazification had come to an end.

Of course, it was quite logical. Where do you find experienced people to run a country who had not done so during the twelve years of the Nazi regime? MG found Konrad Adenauer, who had been Mayor of Cologne and had retired before the Nazis took power, and who therefore was untainted. They made him Chancellor, expecting him to last only a little while because of his age. But he lived on and on and became a great Chancellor.

But how many like him could be found?

If I had ever flirted with the idea of staying on, this incident convinced me not to do so. I did not want to deal with "former" Nazis and help them to resume their positions of authority.

In December of 1945 my number came up. My teammates threw me a farewell party. Late that evening, I got into my BMW and drove to Frankfurt, an hour away, to report to SHAEF in the IG Farben complex for transport home.

I left my BMW in the parking lot with the keys in it. I wonder what ever happened to it.

In its usual hurry up and wait manner, it took the Army four weeks to get me back home.

First, a few days in Frankfurt. Then, transport to Antwerp. A week or so in Antwerp. Finally, aboard ship.

This was also a small troop transport with hammocks five high. This time, we did not have to wear life preservers and there was no convoy. I had to surrender my badge, my identification and the guns that had been issued to me, but I still had the Walther pistol, which had been confiscated and so did not appear on any inventory records.

There was a major Atlantic storm. It was so bad that, as I learned later, the aircraft carrier WASP had been damaged and had to return for repairs. But our ship went on.

I was told that it was illegal to own a gun in New York State, unless the firing pin was destroyed. I did not want to keep a useless pistol as a souvenir, so I sold it to someone from a gun friendly state.

There was a great deal of seasickness during this crossing, but eventually, we landed somewhere in New Jersey and were taken to Fort Dix. Full circle.

There were telephones made available to us, and of course, I called my parents and sister to tell them that I was back and expected to be home in a few days.

Then there was the discharge procedure, which was as complicated as the induction.

Among the various things the Army did for us was the issuance of a small lapel pin, to be worn with civilian clothes, which indicated veteran status. After the first six months only professional veterans continued to wear it. The pin was in the shape of an American Eagle, so naturally, everybody called it the ruptured duck.

By early January of 1946 I came home.

Home was a city I had lived in for two years, in a country I did not know.

For eight years, from the Anschluss to that moment, my life had been dominated by the existence of Nazi Germany and structured by my reaction to it. Now Nazi Germany was gone. The war was over.

I had no idea what I should do with myself. I was terrified.

But everything was possible.

So I began.

ACKNOWLEDGEMENTS

The busiest woman in the world is my daughter Shereen.

She chairs the Cultural Science Department and directs the Honors Program at Mesa Community College, is a wonderful wife and devoted mother to two peripatetic children, and the best daughter any man could hope for.

She is the one who urged me to write my story for the general public. And then she edited and formatted the book, inserted the photographs, and handled all the computer related problems that my generation finds impossible.

If you, Dear Reader, found something of interest in my story, thank her. As for me, I cannot ever thank her enough for deciding to be born my daughter.

And then there is my wife, Lenore, who is also a College Professor and has had to put up with my accent and grammatical errors for many years. Her wise hand in correcting and editing my errors cannot be overpraised.

I am indeed fortunate in having received help from such talented women.